SO-BAR-849

The Book
That Made Me

The Book
That Made Me

edited by Judith Ridge

CANDLEWICK PRESS

For my parents, Edith and Barry Ridge,
for all the love (and books) that made me

Contents

Introduction

Growing up, reading was my first and best thing. I don't remember not being able to read—I was one of those precocious children who was reading before school, reading novels (Enid Blyton's *Adventures of the Wishing-Chair*, to be precise) by the time I was in Year Two. For some people, reading is difficult—for me, it was like osmosis. I just seemed to absorb it into my way of being in the world as soon as was humanly, and cognitively, possible. Any time my family couldn't find me—skiving off from the washing up or just disappeared for hours—they knew that wherever they'd find me, in the loo or up a tree, I'd have a book with me.

For me it was almost always fiction (when it wasn't Archie Comics and *Pink* magazine—an English girls' magazine that published comic strips and preteen-suitable romance stories side by side with profiles of such top 1970s pop stars as the Bay City Rollers, Paper Lace, and the Rubettes. Google them and thank me later). I probably read five or six books a week as a kid, often rereading old favorites multiple times, while falling for new delights borrowed from the school or local library. (Thanks, Auburn Council in Sydney's west—you had the best collection an obsessive reader could have asked for.)

Later in life, though, I've come to equally enjoy memoir—stories of people's lives. Not autobiography, strictly speaking, but slices of lives, especially when they are the memoirs of writers. Writers' memoirs, at their best, provide not merely insights into their childhoods, or romances, or whatever significant moments in their lives they choose to focus on, but often, indeed, almost always, they are meditations on creativity, and the role books and reading have played in the memoirist's life. Memoirs such as Jeanette Winterson's *Why Be Happy When You Could Be Normal?* go so far as to suggest that books, and reading, can not only make a life; they can save it.

This growing fascination with writers' reading lives led me to the creation of this book. I didn't know much about writers when I was a young reader. Apart from a few big names like Enid Blyton, and Ethel Turner, who wrote my beloved *Seven Little Australians* and whose grandchildren holidayed at the same beach we did, authors were simply names on books. Now, of course, writers are celebrities, and their readers often have opportunities to meet them. But still, I wondered, how great would it be for today's young readers to catch a glimpse into the books that helped build the writers they love? Thinking about the writers I knew and loved, I wondered, what was the book that *made* them—the book that made them fall in love, or made them understand something for the first time? Made them think. Made them laugh. Made them angry. Made them feel safe. Made them feel challenged in ways they never knew they could be, emotionally, intellectually, politically. Made them readers, made them writers—made them the person they are today. And so I asked them. The book you hold in your hands is the result.

As you'll see when you start dipping into the essays, poems, memoirs, and other pieces in this collection, there's a fascinating variety of stories told by people who ended up making words and stories their living (and perhaps their life). Some of the books that "made" them were encountered when they were very small children—see Ursula Dubosarsky's charming verse account of her kindergarten readers. Some were primary-school age (as with my own story, recounted below, and James Roy's tribute to the Australian classic children's novel *Josh*). Most, though, were in their teens and ready, as Emily Maguire so perfectly says in her essay about Frank Moorhouse's novel *Grand Days*, for something to smash and explode their mind and their world wide open.

Some of the books you'll read about were in fact comics; some were magazines (stolen, as in Benjamin Law's hilariously cheeky account, from an older sister). Some weren't in paper form at all but were stories passed down through family and culture— Ambelin Kwaymullina for one reminds us of the source of all story, from the oral traditions of our ancestors, wherever we, or they, came from.

Whatever their form, and whatever the age the reader was when they were read, they were all books, stories, or experiences that one way or another changed the reader. For good.

For myself, the book that made me the kind of reader I am and, I suspect, played no small part in my decision to make a life trying to get inside books and figure out how they work, was the first book I ever read that challenged me on an intellectual and, for want of a better word, creative level.

The book was *The Flame Takers,* a novel by the Australian author Lilith Norman. It was published in 1973, and I would have read it that year or a year or two, at most, later. I knew Norman's work well—I'd been reading her for years in the New South Wales *School Magazine,* where she worked on the editorial staff. I'd also read all of her previous novels, all more or less in the realist mode, about recognizably real children in recognizably real places and situations. Her best-known book at the time was probably *Climb a Lonely Hill,* about children stranded in the desert after a car accident. (Surviving the Australian environment was a favorite theme of children's writers of the 1960s and '70s.)

The Flame Takers, though, was something else.

The protagonists are still very real—young teenage brother and sister Mark and Joanna Malory, in their early years of high school at Sydney Boys and Girls High respectively (Norman was a proud alumna of Sydney Girls High School). The narrative begins as Mark's story—he's a gifted musician, the son of theatrical parents and grandparents, all of whose creative talents slowly start being drained away by some unknown, mysterious force. Audaciously, about a third of the way into the novel, Norman switches our attention from Mark to Joanna, the blessedly (so Joanna herself says) untalented member of the family, who is the one left to find the cause of her family's "flames"—their creativity—being lost.

The Flame Takers was the first book I found difficult, whose meaning was slippery and opaque, whose language and story spiraled around me like elusive, elliptical phantoms. It was the first book I remember where the story didn't immediately present itself to me, but where I had to enter into the book in all its strangeness and make my own sense, make my own meaning.

It was the book that introduced me to the intense pleasures of entering deep within the very bones of a story and working out its secrets from the inside out.

And while I may have ended up here anyway, I can't help but think it was *The Flame Takers* that determined my life's path as a student of literature, which led me in time to work as an editor—for many years at *School Magazine,* following in Lilith Norman's remarkable footsteps—and then, in another turn, a teacher of creative writing. Along the way, I've come to know and admire a lot of writers—many of whom are represented in the pages of this book.

We hope that you may find inspiration and challenges to extend and expand your own reading life from the many amazing books written about—and written by—the contributors to *The Book That Made Me.* We've provided a handy list at the back for you, along with information about all the contributors (and, accompanying many of the essays, a sneak peek at their past selves!).

Finally, because everyone involved in this book believes so deeply and determinedly in both the need for and the right of every child to have access to the highest standards of literacy skills possible, so that they, too, can be made (and undone!) by books, all author and anthologist royalties from *The Book That Made Me* will go to Australia's Indigenous Literacy Foundation (ILF). The foundation sends books into Aboriginal and Torres Strait Islander communities—schools and homes—and supports young Indigenous readers by providing books in both Aboriginal (First) languages and English.

Thank you for supporting our support for the ILF, and now, may we present a book that we hope, one way or another, might just also be the making of you.

Judith Ridge

Shaun Tan Asks

WHY DO YOU READ?

let's ask some
random strangers...

I never know what I'll find!

A Feverish Desire to Possess
Randa Abdel-Fattah

I have vivid memories of spending Saturdays with my mother and sister, moving from one wholesale bookseller to another in the suburbs of Melbourne, Australia, in the eighties and early nineties. My mother, a senior teacher and administrator at Australia's first Islamic school, was tasked with building the school's emerging library. As she browsed each warehouse, I would pore over the books lining the shelves in the children's section: the Sweet Dreams series, Sweet Valley High, the Baby-Sitters Club, Nancy Drew, Judy Blume, Robin Klein, R. L. Stine, Christopher Pike, Caroline B. Cooney. My bedroom walls were lined with photocopies I'd made of the covers of the Baby-Sitters Club books (alongside my Kylie Minogue and Michael Jackson posters).

Almost every second Sunday my father would take me to the Caribbean Gardens and Market in the suburb of Scoresby to visit a particular secondhand bookseller who stocked the Sweet Valley High series. I remember the long drive down Spring Valley Road, the anticipation building inside me. What books would I find this weekend? Would I come closer to completing my collection?

The Sweet Valley High series was set in California and offered readers stories about love, friendship, proms, jocks, sibling rivalry, and romance. Girls with names like Jessica and Elizabeth fell for boys with names like Todd, Paul, Bruce, and Michael — boys who had "sandy hair and piercing blue eyes" and were either the "rich boy next door" or a sports coach at a summer camp.

The stories I read filled me with a feverish desire to possess them. I wanted so badly to be part of these books — as their reader, as their writer. The only way of assuaging this desire was to write my own stories. And so I did. My father made me a writing desk, and I threw myself into storytelling. The stories I wrote were all set in America, focusing on scandalous love triangles, sororities and fraternities, tragic tales of running away from home, chaos at school camps, proms, snow fights during school. My characters ate ham-and-cheese sandwiches and snacked on "Twinkies," even though I had no idea what a Twinkie was (these were pre-Google days, after all). Their names were invariably Lisa, Samantha, Liz, or Kylie. They always had blond hair, blue eyes, and milky-white skin. The cliché machine was working overtime.

Why should all of this be so strange?

Because I'm an Australian-born Muslim of Palestinian Egyptian heritage with an unpronounceable surname (the phlegm inflection is necessary), curly dark hair (blow-dried and tamed now but electric power point out-of-control as a kid and teenager), who spent Saturday mornings at Arabic school among boys called Mohamed and Ahmed and girls called Fatma and

Aisha. During the week, I attended a Catholic primary school. It was located in Bulleen, Melbourne, and many of the students were of European extraction, so the boys I spent hours writing "Dear Diary" entries over had names like Nicholas Papadopoulos and Eddie Bonnachi. My school was filled with eucalyptus trees, tanbark, and creepy-crawlies; we had water fights, not snow fights, and we bought our lunch from the tuck shop, not a cafeteria.

Much like the teenage fiction I grew up with, my own Arab and Muslim identity is invisible in my early writing. Although my life offered a potential rich tapestry of racial tropes and ethnic fetishisms—the stock-standard roles of cabdriver, convenience store owner, terrorist or tyrant, oppressed Muslim woman—I couldn't manage to exploit them for the purposes of telling a good yarn. To think I could have written the habib version of Sweet Valley High, set in Bankstown, Sydney, featuring twins Fatima and Jamilah. Sadly, my characters' names were all pronounceable, everybody's hair was Brylcreem-free, and lunch consisted of sliced white bread, not kebab leftovers that stank up the locker room. (*Oh, Mum, what were you thinking?*)

The absence of diversity in the popular fiction I grew up with was, I believe, symptomatic of a collective imagination that equates mainstream with Anglo, and that casts indigenous people, minorities, and migrants as exotic, fascinating deviations from the norm.

The only exception to this that I can recall from the childhood books I read is Claudia Kishi in the Baby-Sitters Club. Subverting stereotypes, Claudia is Japanese American and—wait for it—not academically inclined! Claudia was perhaps one of the first encounters I had with a non-Anglo character who did not reinforce popular stereotypes. While this was perhaps not a particularly sophisticated example of antiracism politics, it should be credited as insightful given the time and context.

And then, against this backdrop of Anglo-centric fiction, came along a book that turned my life upside down. Aged thirteen, my "coming of age" coincided with a particularly difficult time for my minority community: the first Gulf War, which began in 1990. Australia, supporting the United States, deployed warships to the Gulf. In the public imagination, Arab Australians and Muslims were suddenly cast as the archetypal folk devils, made to feel like outsiders and suspicious Others because of events overseas over which they had no control. It was assumed that all Arabs and Muslims in Australia supported Saddam Hussein and that their loyalty to Australia was therefore in doubt. Media representations insisted on representing Muslims and Arabs in homogenous, monolithic terms, associating Islam with violence, fanaticism, and fundamentalism. I felt this personally. Identified as a Muslim by the hijab I wore, I was called a wog, terrorist, nappy-head, camel jockey, and sand nigger. My faith and identity were the subjects of interrogation and discipline. I was spat at on the street and told to "go back home." (*Postcode 3109, morons,* I would yell back.) When you're thirteen and feel as though you're locked up in a cage of other people's demonizing rhetoric, totalizing assumptions, and crude stereotypes, your already precarious sense of identity and belonging threatens to unravel. You are made to walk the plank—a plank hitched up by people who politicize your very existence at a time when you simply want to get on with the business of being a teenager and worry about acne and schoolgirl crushes and big dreams and fierce friendships.

I poured myself into books, searching for escapism. I did not dare to hope for validation, a cultural point of reference that spoke to me and all the identity hyphens I straddled.

And then I read Melina Marchetta's *Looking for Alibrandi*.

There are books you read that make you hold your breath. It's only when you get to the end that you realize you need to come up for air. In fact, the origins of the word *inspiration* stem from the act of inhaling. There is something sensuous and visceral in the experience of being inspired. I felt it with *Looking for Alibrandi*.

I read it in one sitting. And then I read it again. And again. Something inside me changed.

For the very first time in my own life, there was a book that didn't fetishize a migrant upbringing. Josie wasn't somebody to pity or consider "exotic." I identified with her world, the pressures and challenges of straddling what I considered at that age to be identities in competition with each other. I loved Josie's gutsiness, her insistence on making up her own mind about sex and not giving in to peer pressure. I loved her loud, vibrant, complicated family, and the fact that her experiences with racism vindicated my own. Even the cover appealed to me. Defying the quintessential blond and blue-eyed Aussie girl, *this* girl had long, dark, curly hair and olive skin. Believe me, this was no small matter. I regularly placed my head on the ironing board and allowed my friends to iron my hair (risking scalp burns and singed locks) in a perennial effort to attain smooth hair. Sun-In (a spray-on hair lightener) was also a popular choice among my friends at the time and allowed one to circumvent the parental prohibition against hair dye by spraying the hair to lighten it (my hijab served more than just a spiritual function; it also allowed me to conceal evidence). Here was Josie with curly hair and not an iron or Sun-In spray bottle to be seen.

I couldn't believe I'd opened a young adult book that spoke to my life. It was wildly empowering and gratifying, especially because the author was of Italian background. While I had always wanted to be a writer, the stories I was dabbling with continued to be set in American or English towns and cities. Although I'd graduated to writing mysteries involving kidnappings and murdered friends, a prom or an English boarding school always managed to slip its way in. I was writing stories about white people, for white people, and as if I was a white person. Was it possible that my own story might have some worth?

Above all else, this is what Melina Marchetta offered me: a lightbulb moment, illuminating crevices and corners of my imagination and creativity that had been kept in the dark. The books I'd read had socialized me into subconsciously discounting my story. Suddenly I realized that my own experiences just might matter.

And so it is perhaps no surprise that when I set out to write my own novel based on my own experiences at the age of fifteen, I placed *Looking for Alibrandi* in a prominent position on my desk. Whenever I felt weary of my writing, lost confidence in my voice, and felt plagued by self-doubt, *Alibrandi* would gently remind me to celebrate my identity and seize the chance to insist on an alternative story, one told on my terms and through my own agency. And for that I am indebted to Melina Marchetta, who, in bringing Josie to life, in some way managed to do the same to my story, too.

I'm a bookworm.
What more do you need to know?

Twelve Reasons
Markus Zusak

Twelve Reasons why *The Outsiders* by S. E. Hinton is one of the books that made me *me:*

1. It has a great first line, about dark and light and Paul Newman, so how can you go wrong?

2. It's about brothers, and about boys who behave like brothers.

3. The Greasers have ridiculously outlandish names, like Sodapop, Ponyboy, and Two-Bit.

4. There's danger and love and fighting and caring—just like there is in all of us.

5. Diane Lane is magnificent as Cherry Valance in the movie (way better than Cruise, Dillon, Lowe, and Swayze combined).

6. It differentiates between the meaning of something that's *tough* and something that's *tuff*. (That said, I'm still trying to figure it out.)

7. It led to even better books by S. E. Hinton, like *Tex* and especially *Rumble Fish*—which in my mind is her greatest book, or, actually, a ninety-two-page masterpiece.

8. S. E. Hinton was seventeen years old when the book was published, which made me believe, when I was seventeen, that *I* could be a writer too.

9. For two decades now, certain friends and I still tell each other to *stay gold*—just for laughs (but deep down we really mean it).

10. The toughest greaser, Dallas Winston, is a great antihero.

11. When I was fourteen, I stayed up all night in my yellow-lit bedroom to finish reading this book. It bothered the hell out of my brother on the other side of the room—but I couldn't have cared less.

12. (And most important . . .) After I read this book, for the longest time, I wanted to be Ponyboy.

I like books about ponies.
You gotta problem with that?

A Short Leap
Cathy Cassidy

I learned to love reading early on. When I was six, our teacher walked a class of forty small children on a ten-minute trip to the local library; we got a guided tour, someone read us a story, and on the way out we were each given a library ticket.

I told my parents this at teatime that day, and Dad's face lit up. Half an hour later we were driving back to that library together, to choose books in what was to become a regular routine. We had no bookshelves at home, so the books piled up in heaps on the floor, and occasionally my mum tidied them away into a cupboard under the stairs. Dad and I widened our net, and the weekly library forays began to take in two more local libraries; my mum and brother didn't share our love of reading, so we managed to get library tickets in their names so we could borrow still more books.

I loved reading, but even so, the only books I actually owned were the occasional Christmas annual.

Then, the year I turned twelve, something amazing happened. I was given a book, and it wasn't an annual or a book of nursery rhymes or fairy tales, but a real novel. The book was *Watership Down* by Richard Adams.

I was amazed. It wasn't my birthday, it wasn't Christmas . . . and yet here was a book, a perfect, awesome book with small print and endless chapters and the promise of escapism and magic. The book even had an amazing cover, a low-key illustrated image of a rabbit with a landscape of hills and downs behind. I loved rabbits, so that was a plus point. Suddenly, I could see the world from their perspective, imagine myself in a whole different world. . . . *Watership Down* is a real adventure story about a group of rabbits who escape to seek a new home when one of them senses that danger is coming; their journey is exciting and difficult, and they outwit humans and make enemies before finally establishing a better future.

The story pulled me in at once. Like all the best books, this glued itself to my hands, and I couldn't put it down all weekend. I was miles away, with a big bunch of rabbits, in the middle of a brilliant adventure. On Monday morning I couldn't bear the idea of leaving the book behind, so I sneaked it into my schoolbag.

There was just one problem. I was twelve, and in the second year of a pretty tough secondary school where reading was not always considered to be cool. None of my friends were bookworms, and the idea of being caught reading a book with a big picture of a rabbit on the cover was my worst nightmare. People would laugh and call me a bookworm—worse, they'd think I was a baby, reading a book about rabbits. *Watership Down* was probably the most grown-up book I'd read up to that point, not babyish at all, but my classmates might not know that.

In the end, the need to keep on reading won out, and I headed off to school with the book hidden away under my school stuff. I was hoping to find a quiet moment to myself to read in peace, although in a big rowdy school like ours that wasn't very likely. Maybe on the bus coming home?

Finally, I struck lucky. Our English teacher was late coming to class, and my friends gathered in a noisy, gossipy knot outside the classroom door, making the most of the unexpected freedom. Instead of joining them, I headed in the opposite direction and found a quiet corner with a radiator where I could lean and read in peace, all at a safe distance from my classmates.

I opened up the book, taking great care to place a hand over the embarrassing rabbit picture on the cover, and right away I was tugged back into the story, battling life and death with Hazel, Fiver, Bigwig, and Kehaar.

Then, the worst thing I could have imagined happened. The coolest boy in our year walked up to me and said, "What are you reading?" He had never even looked at me before, let alone spoken to me. My face was crimson with shame, but I had no choice but to show him the book.

"*Watership Down* is the best book I've ever read," he said.

I was speechless. All that worrying . . . and instead of being laughed at or picked on, I'd made a new friend, someone who loved reading just as much as I did.

That book and that incident will always stay in my head, because I learned a huge lesson, one that I should have known all along. Reading is cool—no matter what. No need to feel shy about it, no need to explain your choice of book, no need to panic and assume people won't understand: reading is a magic carpet that can take you anywhere and everywhere, the perfect way to escape a less-than-perfect life. As soon as I worked that out, it was just a short leap to realizing that creating my own stories was possible too . . . and a whole different world opened up to me.

Watership Down . . . the book that made me understand why we need the magic of stories, and why we should never, ever be ashamed of that.

I'm researching Ancient Roman bloodsports!

"What Happens Next?"
Will Kostakis

I should probably start by saying I don't know how much of this is true.

It started off as true, but like all the stories I keep repeating, it's grown with each telling, reshaped by six years of audience reaction. Now, it lies somewhere between "Will taking creative license" and "Will padding a little kernel of truth with a whole lot of fiction."

But that doesn't change that little kernel of truth: I am here, I am who I am, with the career that I have, because of one book: *Hatchet* by Gary Paulsen.

Don't get me wrong, there was a trail of books that inspired me before *Hatchet* fell into my lap halfway through Year Six. Enid Blyton lit a spark with her Faraway Tree adventures, and Morris Gleitzman fanned it into a flame with consistent, awe-inspiring brilliance. But none of them had the impact that *Hatchet* did.

And full disclosure, I only read about six pages.

Each day, my Year Six teacher, Mr. Tait, set fifteen minutes aside after recess for silent reading. He would select a book, and over the course of a term, we would read it at our own pace. *Hatchet* was his latest selection. Since my parents' divorce was fairly recent and fairly volatile, I had expected to connect with *Hatchet*. It opened with thirteen-year-old Brian in a light plane en route to his father's, where he'd be spending the summer.

Great. I was familiar with the every-second-weekend song and dance. I was totally on board.

Then Brian mentioned the hatchet his mother gave him as a going-away present. Now, my mum wasn't a big fan of my dad, but she'd never stood at the door on one of his Fridays and said, "Oh, and by the way, here's an *axe* in case you . . . you know."

Sure, now as an adult, I can see the perfectly valid reasons for giving Brian an axe. I mean, he'd be spending the summer with his father in the Canadian wilderness. But back then I just couldn't relate to it. I didn't consider all those trees that could be chopped down for firewood. Instead, my mind wandered. . . . I asked myself, why would author Gary Paulsen give his main character an axe? And why would anyone let a thirteen-year-old take it on board a plane rather than force him to stow it with his luggage?

The answers trickled in. Maybe the plane was going to crash. Maybe he'd be the sole survivor. Maybe he'd be left to fend for himself in the harsh wilderness with only an axe.

I brushed my concerns aside. There was no way the story was going to be *that* predictable. I flicked ahead. The pilot had a heart attack, he died, the plane crash-landed, and Brian was left to fend for himself.

I put the book down. Now, I was a big reader, and I had never encountered a book I didn't like before. And while I know now that it's unfair to judge *Hatchet* after six pages, as an eleven-year-old I felt quite passionate about not reading a seventh. I had seen the author working. I had pulled back the curtain and spotted the Wizard.

And I didn't want to read it anymore.

It was a new feeling for me. I had never not done what Mr. Tait told me to. I was eager to please (nauseatingly so), and I took pride in not only doing what I was told, but doing it first.

I glanced around the room. The hatchet hadn't seemed to bother anyone else. Some kids had even made a start on the questions we'd been given on the first chapter.

I knew that if I sat there doing nothing, I'd get into trouble, so I reached for a pen. *Hatchet* hadn't reflected back my experiences as a "child from a broken home," so I decided to start a story that did. I had recently met my father's new girlfriend. It was the first time one of my parents was game enough to introduce me to a prospective partner. It was weird and awkward, for my brothers and me at least; Dad was comfortable enough to pursue the world record for most public displays of affection in one day.

So I wrote about that.

I only managed a few paragraphs before the end of reading time.

The next day, when the rest of the class cracked open their copies of *Hatchet*, I propped mine open in front of me and continued working on my story. I got to the bottom of the page. To everybody watching, I had just finished writing a very detailed response to *Hatchet*'s first chapter.

Well, to almost everybody.

"What are you writing?" Ben, the kid sitting next to me, asked.

Before I could answer, he'd snatched the paper out from under my pen and started reading. He chuckled when he got to the description of Dad playing tonsil tennis with his new girlfriend in the first paragraph. He tsk-tsked sarcastically every time he came to a rude word. He got to the end of the page and checked the back. There was no more.

"What happens next?" he asked.

I hadn't really thought about it. The looming threat of our teacher inspecting our English books had me reconsidering my whole not-reading-*Hatchet* stance.

"Well, tomorrow I wanna read page two," he said.

The next day, I slid page two over to him. I started writing a third without him demanding it.

Then the boy beside Ben asked him what he was reading.

And since we were in Year Six and he hadn't mastered the art of subtlety, Ben said, "I'm reading this," and passed the story along. I was too busy writing to worry about getting caught, but I probably should have put the kibosh on people sharing it around, because a few silent reading times later, when my teacher looked up from his marking, no one in the back row was reading *Hatchet*. Instead, they were passing around my story, one sheet at a time, arguing about who got to read the next page first.

Naturally, Mr. Tait was annoyed, and when he asked who'd written it, naturally, everybody pointed the finger at me.

Mr. Tait collected the story and I got a stern "Kostakis, my office, tomorrow morning."

I got surnamed. I had *never* been surnamed. Only the kids who were in serious trouble got surnamed. I didn't get much sleep that night. I was certain this was it, the end of the road — I was getting expelled. Every rude word, every gut-churning description of my father's disgusting PDAs, all of it flashed before my eyes. Mr. Tait had read *that*.

Yep. Expelled.

The next morning, I was summoned into Mr. Tait's office. My story was stacked on his desk.

He sighed. "William, I read your story. . . ."

Expelled. Definitely expelled.

He leaned in closer. "So . . . what happens next?"

I went to protest, convince him I wasn't worth expelling, but I stopped. I wasn't expelled. He'd asked what happened next. He'd liked the story. He wanted more. And I seized the opportunity.

"Sir, I don't know. It's hard to write this *and* read *Hatchet*," I said.

It was deviously manipulative and it worked. Mr. Tait suggested that instead of reading *Hatchet*, I finish my story. I did, all twenty pages of it. At the end of Year Six, he suggested that I spend my first year of high school trying to turn it into a novel. I did that too. My first rejection letter from a publisher soon followed.

The story grew and changed as I did. I cut out parts to make way for new life experiences as I lived them. Each year, I submitted the finished product, and each year, I was rejected.

But the nature of the rejections changed. The two-sentence "Please never, ever submit to us again" replies slowly became "It's promising, but our manuscript assessor has suggested you look at x, y, and z." In Year Twelve, I got a yes.

By that stage, the manuscript bore little resemblance to the story I had started in Year Six. It was about a group of teenagers who signed up to star in a reality TV show. But beneath *that*, there was still the desire to reflect my own experiences as a child with divorced parents. And even after all those years, and all those edits, I managed to keep the scene with the super-awkward PDAs between a father and his lady friend that I first wrote in Year Six.

Because of *Hatchet*. When we talk about the benefits of reading, we tend to only talk about the books we love, but the books we don't enjoy, those we don't connect with, can be just as beneficial. They tell us about ourselves, our tastes and our limits (an axe on a plane is apparently where I draw the line). The trick is to not let them push us off the bandwagon, to not let them curb our love of reading.

So if nothing speaks to you, then pick up a pen and speak for yourself. Yours may be the voice that someone else is looking for.

I like urban paranormal Victorian
steampunk speculative romance.
A lot more than your dumb questions.

The Great Sense of Unease
Mandy Hager

I think it's fair to say that I'm obsessed with politics and social justice. Don't get me wrong: I hate the games politicians play to score points against their opponents—a kind of verbal bullying, often sexist, sometimes racist, and always designed to deflect away from serious issues that affect you and me. No, the kind of politics I find so fascinating and important is the big-picture stuff: Who is holding all the power and control, how do they get to hold it and maintain it, and whose interests do they have at heart?

I'm what those who don't share my particular views on the world might call a "bleeding-heart leftie"—probably adding "greenie" too. The joke is that they think this is insulting me, while, instead, I wear such labels with pride!

Let's break it down to see what an accusation like that is really saying. "Bleeding heart" to me equals someone who is able to empathize with others, who hurts when they hurt, who feels their sorrows, pains, and losses. "Leftie" equals "left wing"—and *that* means I believe in sharing wealth throughout the whole of a society, not hoovering it all up so it only goes to a few rich guys at the top. And "greenie," well, that's a no-brainer! It means caring about the health and future of our planet (and *everything* that lives on it, not just us).

How did I come to hold such strong (some would say stroppy) views? I guess the same way *you* developed your views. It's a blend of how I was raised and by whom, where and what era I was born, and what I have learned (and read) since then.

You see, my father was half Jewish, born in Austria before the Second World War. If he and my grandparents had not escaped to New Zealand, they would probably have ended up among the millions of people Hitler killed, as many others in my father's extended family did. My mother came from the other side of the world too. She was born in Zanzibar, a tiny island off the coast of East Africa, which was once an important stopover for the slave trade. She watched missionaries handing out Bibles to African kids who couldn't speak English and hadn't been taught to read anyway, and she thought this was ridiculous—especially when there were so many other things that could have improved their lives in much more practical ways, such as better health care, fresh running water, fair pay, proper housing, food, education . . . She saw racism and the damage caused by colonization firsthand and didn't like it, not one little bit.

From as far back as I can remember, my siblings and I were encouraged to stand up for the underdog and for the values that make up a decent society, such as fairness, equality, respect, generosity, sharing, honesty, integrity, compassion, and active engagement in the democratic process. Not hard to understand why, when my parents had both seen such terrible injustices done in their lifetimes. The first protest I can remember being involved in, I was maybe six or seven. We stood in front of bulldozers to prevent them from cutting down a stand of beautiful native trees on the land next door to our house. (Sadly, we didn't win, but that didn't deter us from trying again, and again, for many other causes through the years.) We were encouraged to speak out, to question, to demand the best possible behavior and decision-making from those in charge. Politics was often the subject of discussions around our dinner table (yes, we actually sat down and ate dinner together instead of watching TV!), and my parents modeled their beliefs through action. We opened our home to pregnant unmarried mothers whose families had rejected them, to gay people at a time when being gay was still illegal, and hosted kids from children's homes and reformatories on weekend outings so they could feel part of a loving family, if only for a day.

This was back in the 1960s and 1970s (I know, way back before they knew the earth was round!), and by the time I reached adolescence, I was very much aware of what was going on around me. Nuclear proliferation was a terrifying reality. The Vietnam War was spurring violent protests all over the world. Ireland was in the midst of its bloody civil war, as were many other countries around the globe.

It was around this time, perhaps when I was fourteen or fifteen, that I first read George Orwell's classic novel *Nineteen Eighty-Four*, originally published in 1949. Orwell wrote the book after having observed the atrocities of the Spanish Civil War, the ugly buildup to the Second World War, and the unfolding horror of the Holocaust. Events such as these so disturbed and disgusted him, he made a conscious decision to use his writing as a means of revealing injustice and exposing crimes against humanity, with a personal creative goal of making political writing function as art as well.

Of course he wasn't alone in this. Literary greats like William Shakespeare often focused on the lusts that drove men to do evil (*The evil that men do lives after them; the good is oft interred with their bones*); poets often slay us with their potent insights, from the war poets like Siegfried Sassoon (in particular his poem "Attack") to dreadlocked performance poets like Benjamin Zephaniah ("Save Our Sons [SOS]"). Kurt Vonnegut's *Slaughterhouse-Five* brought the firebombing of Dresden into stark relief, and who could read Suzanne Collins's Hunger Games trilogy without reflecting on the brutality of the politics behind it? Visual artists also used their creativity to make a point; from Pablo Picasso's magnificent painting *Guernica* as a response to the Spanish Civil War (like Orwell), to British artist Banksy's graffiti on the dividing wall between Israel and Palestine, these works are hugely affecting and arresting, all with something worthwhile to say.

Even now, more than a decade into the twenty-first century, *Nineteen Eighty-Four* is terrifying—perhaps more so today than ever before. It's one of the original dystopian novels, setting out a world in a state of perpetual war, where an all-seeing government uses mass surveillance and the manipulation of language and media to control the masses, in order to keep them in a state of docile ignorance. They also heartlessly destroy anyone who dares to stand out as an individual or speak against those in control. This is the book that coined the phrase *Big Brother is watching you*. It is the ultimate reality TV show. A textbook for terrorists of the mind.

What is really so brilliant about this book (and also most terrifying) is that it could just as well have been written last week about what is going on in our world right now, or back in the mid-1970s, when I first read it, as easily as when Orwell wrote it, after the end of the Second World War.

I can remember the great sense of unease I felt knowing that the year 1984 was not some vague imagined "future" but was coming up fast, and that what Orwell was describing was already coming true before my eyes. When we reached 1984 (I was twenty-four years old) I also remember thinking we had dodged a bullet, that it wasn't really that bad.... But, now, thinking about this book again, I'm sad to say that we were living then, as we are living now, in its midst.

This is the magic of truly great fiction: it can either provide a *mirror* in which to reflect what is going on (in ourselves or our world) or it can become a *window* (to see into a life or a world other than our own). In *Nineteen Eighty-Four*'s case, it does both.

George Orwell wrote a brilliant essay called "Why I Write" in which he explained that one of his motivations for writing was "political purpose," going on to say that this means:

Using the word "political" in the widest possible sense. Desire to push the world in a certain direction, to alter other peoples' idea of the kind of society that they should strive after. Once again, no book is genuinely free from political bias. The opinion that art should have nothing to do with politics is itself a political attitude.

When I first read this, I let out a big "YES!" Orwell had voiced exactly what I felt: that politics is at the center of our behaviors, either individually or collectively, and *this* is what I want to write about, *this* is what I care about, *this* is what I want to form the basis of everything I'm trying to say!

This doesn't mean that I want each book to be a lecture or a party political broadcast! But, given that writing a book is such hard work, I figure I may as well spend the time working on something that I really care about and that hopefully has something worthwhile to say. For me, the books (and films and paintings) that I most love are the ones that raise questions inside me and make me think really hard about the issues raised. They might bring to life a person who is struggling with a situation I didn't know existed, so I can feel how it is for them (the window), or they might pit the character up against some situation that reflects some issue in my own world (the mirror) and, in the process, clarifies how I feel about it.

The other thing a good book has to do, in my opinion, is to move me emotionally. It needs to grab me by the heart and make me ache for the character as if they were a part of me. To me, this is what makes a piece of writing powerful: that ability to tap straight into a reader's heart. George Orwell's *Nineteen Eighty-Four* does this brilliantly, by showing us the most intimate parts of main character Winston Smith's life, so that when they come for him (as they always come for those who stray from the official line in totalitarian societies), we feel his terror and slow destruction and it feeds our outrage.

This word *outrage* is a really important one. It is often what finally feeds action — and without action to back up outrage, nothing ever changes. I actively want to make change for the better in my world. George Orwell thought the same. That's why I admire him — not only for the brilliance of his writing, but also for his determination to stand up for what he believed in. To try to make a difference. To give another voice to those whose voices have been stifled.

So, if you only read one book this year, try reading *Nineteen Eighty-Four*—and think about how we let the world get into such a mess, and what part you can take in helping to change it. One of the characters in *Nineteen Eighty-Four* says: "Until they become conscious they will never rebel, and until after they have rebelled they cannot become conscious." I say, rebel and be conscious! Let's all have a damn good stab at proving him wrong and making sure his dystopia can be forgotten as we work to build a new utopia instead!

I love all your
crazy Earthling antics!

Hooked (and a Bit Unsettled)
Shaun Tan

I ought to begin this list of recommended children's books with an early "mistake" made by my mother when it came to bedtime reading. She herself did not grow up in a literary household: as a kid I was almost fascinated by the sheer absence of books, or even paper and pencils, in my grandparents' house; it just wasn't really part of their world. Perhaps for this reason, our mum felt her own children should be exposed to as many books as possible, but at the same time was not guided by either experience or the kinds of "recommended reading" lists you can find on websites today. If it looked vaguely interesting, Mum would read it to my brother and me at bedtime. One such title read to us around the ages of seven and eight was an apparently charming fairy tale by some guy named George Orwell:

Mr. Jones, of the Manor Farm, had locked the hen-houses for the night, but was too drunk to remember to shut the pop-holes....

I think we were all hooked (and a bit unsettled) from the outset, so there was no turning back. My brother and I looked forward to each progressively disturbing chapter: conniving pigs, brainwashed sheep, a horse carted off to something called a "knackers," and poor Mum had to field all of our questions. I asked her recently about this, and she remembers being increasingly anxious as the book went on about how this "might affect our young minds"—yet we voted to keep going. (Bedtime reading should always be democratic.) Of course the book ends with all the pigs celebrating their triumphant depravity, and our Mum was *very* worried about that. For my part, as a kid, I just thought it was terrific. And it was no more disturbing than stuff I witnessed at school every day, with its occasionally cruel kids and less-than-perfect teachers—I thought Orwell was right on the money. (The whole Soviet satire thing was something I found out about much later.)

I'd never thought about a story so much after it was read, and from then on, I really appreciated unresolved endings, in contrast to all the other less-convincing moralizing stuff that kids were being regularly fed in suburban Australia. I also realized books weren't just for entertainment. *Animal Farm* (along with *Watership Down* and *Gulliver's Travels*) certainly later influenced my development as an author and illustrator, which may be obvious with books such as *The Rabbits*, a fairly confronting allegory about colonization written by John Marsden. Interestingly, that was quite a controversial book when published (banned in some Australian schools), yet even very young children seem to enjoy and understand it quite deeply, and grasp the hidden optimism that adults sometimes miss. That continues to be very surprising—children's ability to find positive linings in grim stories.

My interest in picture books really only came about as an adult artist, moving from painting into commercial illustration and looking for interesting work. Until very recently I haven't had children, or spent much time with them, and don't specifically write/paint for children. Maybe that's why kids like my work! I just think of them as smallish people who are very smart and creative and pretty honest in their opinions. So when I think about favorite children's books, I tend to think about any good book that has the widest possible readership—from toddlers to geriatrics—and can be understood on many different levels. Picture books are great for this, because they are concise, easily reread several times, and often invent their own narrative grammar, as if you are learning how to read all over again.

One of the books that got me quite interested professionally, thinking, "I'd really love to do something like that one day," is *Fish in the Sky* by George Mendoza, illustrated by designer Milton Glaser. (Even if you don't know Glaser's work, you almost certainly do, from his colorful Bob Dylan profile to the "I heart NY" logo.) I originally saw this out-of-print book reproduced as tiny images in one of Glaser's retrospective books on graphic design, while researching much more "serious" stuff as a fine arts undergrad. It's a series of poetic metaphors, illustrated in a fairly indirect and slightly surrealist way. An image of a big yellow flower floating in the middle of a room is particularly resonant, as the book is about both the power and fragility of sensory memory—no particular narrative as such. This approach has increasingly interested me as a "visual writer," and *Fish in the Sky* strongly influenced my own picture book about depression, *The Red Tree*.

The Mysteries of Harris Burdick by Chris Van Allsburg, originally published in 1984. I came across a copy in my outer-suburban library in Western Australia (authors should always be aware that their work ends up in the most far-flung places!), and thought, "This is weird—where's the story?" before putting it back. But my ten-year-old curiosity kept me returning, and I soon appreciated the genius of Van Allsburg's approach to storytelling: let the reader do all the work! *Mysteries* is a series of fragments, stories that might have been, but represented by only a singular image, a title, and a dislocated sentence. Even the absence of color (it's all black and white) only adds to the atmospheric allure of each quiet enigma: a nun floating on an airborne chair, a lump under the carpet, an ocean liner forcing its way into a tiny canal, a house enjoying a "perfect lift-off." You can't help but imagine your own story in each case: it's almost impossible not to think creatively. And this book reminds us of what is so special about books—that the reader is a co-creator of the world, not just a recipient; they are the principal director of an author's screenplay and illustrator's concept art. I think that's a key realization to being a good writer or illustrator—creative humility. You should never feel smarter than your audience.

On the subject of influence, I'll list a few other notables that hooked me around the time I was a largely unemployed freelancer, looking for inspiration: Lane Smith's illustrations for *The Stinky Cheese Man and Other Fairly Stupid Tales, When the Wind Blows* by Raymond Briggs, *Starry Messenger* by Peter Sís, *Free Lunch* by Vivian Walsh and J. Otto Seibold. These books really opened my mind to the sophistication and potential—and craziness—of picture books, a form I'd largely dismissed since childhood as kids' stuff. They were intriguing, original, funny, and as complex as any other work of art.

Australia has a particularly strong picture book culture. Ron Brooks is one of my favorite illustrators, and I'd recommend his book *Fox* with Margaret Wild, a terrific picture book writer not afraid to tackle big subjects. This very universal fable has a touch of Orwell about it: half-blind Dog rescues crippled Magpie, and together they help each other survive in the bush—until lonely Fox comes along to lure Magpie away. Yet Fox doesn't want to befriend her or even eat her. He just wants her and Dog to know what loneliness is like. It's gut-wrenching stuff, and could only ever achieve full impact as a short, seemingly innocent-looking picture book. Children, of course, know all about this kind of social carnage, and no doubt enjoy seeing it represented honestly as much as adults do.

Along similar lines is Armin Greder's *The Island*, about a stranger washed ashore on an island of gossipy villagers. They take him in but become increasingly afraid of his "ominous" presence, even though the man does not say or do anything. The story cuts to the core of so many contemporary debates about refugees, particularly here in Australia, a very big island with a very checkered history when it comes to immigration. Greder's drawings, like those of Ron Brooks, convey a good part of the story through a quiet and expressive "ugly beauty."

Okay, these are all pretty dark books, which may only reflect my particular inclination, e.g., loving Edward Gorey's *The Gashlycrumb Tinies* (an alphabet book of Victorian children meeting their end in novel ways) and the book I checked out the most times at my local library as a kid, *The Headless Horseman Rides Tonight: More Poems to Trouble Your Sleep* by Jack Prelutsky and Arnold Lobel. So to balance this out a bit, I'd recommend some lighter fun in Leigh Hobbs's *Mr Chicken Goes to Paris*. Often when I'm with friends, we will joke about absurd scenarios or verbal nonsense that, while hilarious, will go no further than the dinner table. But if you are someone like Hobbs, it's all grist to the mill. His drawings look very much like dinner-napkin doodles, with a healthy disregard for continuity or finesse. Mr. Chicken is something like a defrosted supermarket chicken with an angry face, fangs, and — as described in his passport — "everything yellow." He's also gigantic: a monster with a parson's nose — as an actual nose. But he has a friend called Yvonne in Paris, a happy little girl who takes him on a sightseeing tour . . . and that's pretty much it! What makes Hobbs's work funny is that everything is so understated and matter-of-fact, and there's something quite Australian about this sort of surreal laconic humor. It's a quality also present in another of my favorite picture books, *The Great Escape from City Zoo* by Tohby Riddle. It's about four animals on the run who manage to hold regular jobs and apartments in a city like New York, where people are most likely to overlook the fact that you are actually a flamingo or an ant-eater, so long as you keep your clothes on and pay your taxes. Just don't fall on your back if you're a turtle or faint outside a taxidermist's shop window. Then the ruse is up.

So there are some good picture books; there are of course many more. My own working practice has more recently drifted into the gray area between picture books and comics, so I've been reading a lot of graphic novels, which also inform my work as a filmmaker. It's "gray" partly because of blurry definition boundaries — panels, pages, word bubbles — but also because the audience can be hard to pick, though they are often more "young adult" than children's books. But again, the best ones are perhaps those that cross over, and here I would include Raymond Briggs, particularly *The Snowman* (which greatly influenced my own book *The Arrival*) and the biography of his parents, *Ethel & Ernest: A True Story*. Gene Luen Yang's *American Born Chinese* was personally very resonant for me: as an Australian-born half-Chinese growing up in a very non-Asian place, I recognized a lot of Yang's neuroses (also dealt with in the work of Adrian Tomine — *Shortcomings* — whose very faulty protagonists look eerily just like me! I have to ask him about that one day). *Skim* by Canadian cousins Jillian and Mariko Tamaki deals with some similar themes from a female perspective, plus a whole lot of other teenage angst, perfectly pitched. In fact, a big theme of many graphic novels is marginality — where the medium and message have a bit in common: *Stitches* by David Small, *Blankets* by Craig Thompson, *Ghost World* by Daniel Clowes, *Persepolis* by Marjane Satrapi. All about individuals looking for meaning in a confusing, troubled world — which certainly describes my own work too. What's great at the moment is the sheer diversity of work being produced — a good graphic novel can come from anywhere, be created by anyone (with enough patience), and be about anything.

I guess we may see even more interesting things with the development of e-books, but returning to the traditional picture book — words and images printed on a few pieces of paper — it's a pretty timeless format and hard to beat. Books are actually objects, and that's a big part of their appeal. Their physical limitation also inspires much creative problem-solving too — my best work grows out of formal restrictions. I've dabbled with a lot of other things but always seem to come back to picture books as a perfect vehicle for creating very simple, complex little worlds that everyone can enjoy and easily revisit at different times in their life.

Thwack!
Fiona Wood

By the age of ten I was addicted to books and reading. E. Nesbit, Joan Aiken, Enid Blyton, Noel Streatfeild, C. S. Lewis, and Louisa May Alcott were among my favorite writers. But if I had to choose just one book from that time, it would be L. M. Montgomery's *Anne of Green Gables*, which I reread at least six times between the ages of ten and thirteen.

Eight extremely useful things I learned from *Anne of Green Gables* when I was ten:

1. Love is definitely a thing and some people speak about it.

More than anything, *Anne of Green Gables* is about love and its transformative power. It's the story of Anne Shirley, an orphan, who is adopted when she is eleven by sister and brother Marilla and Matthew, both in their late middle age. They were hoping for a boy to help with farmwork, but instead, through a mistaken message, take delivery of a curious, imaginative, passionate girl who has a great hunger to love and to be loved. Through the adoption, Anne is, ostensibly, the character with the most to gain. But the story is as much about the transformation of the lives of Marilla and Matthew as it is of Anne's.

Anne's effusive expression of love counterbalances Marilla's inability to articulate her own feelings, and Matthew's understated tenderness.

Marilla would have given much just then to have possessed Anne's power of putting her feelings into words; but nature and habit had willed it otherwise, and she could only put her arms close about her girl and hold her tenderly to her heart, wishing that she need never let her go.

When I was a child, nobody spoke of love. It wasn't the done thing in my family, and perhaps such reticence was typical of the time. I had clothes, a roof over my head, food on the table, and my mother tucked me into bed at night—so I could certainly infer a level of care and support. It was not an era of praise or affirmation, either. And I was given short shrift if I ever said I was scared. In fact, emotion of any description called for control, not expression. Much of what I knew about love, at ten, I learned from books.

2. Daydreaming is good for you.

Anne is drawn as an imaginative and responsive character. She apprehends the world with the aesthetic appreciation of an artist. She is frequently lost in a reverie of one sort or another—and so was I. Daydreaming was not well received in my world. At home, where it was called "moping about," I'd be told to go outside and play; at school it meant being in trouble for not paying attention, so the representation of Anne's musings provided a comforting affirmation that daydreaming was okay.

I wonder how I would have responded to some of the rapturous descriptions of the natural world, or the more whimsical metaphors L. M. Montgomery gives to Anne, had I first encountered them as an older reader. I'll never know; I have just reread the book alongside my ten-year-old self, who loves that rapture and whimsy unreservedly, and always will. In the same moment I reexperience, and I am nostalgic for, my innocent first readings; the echo brings tears to my eyes.

3. Your kindred spirits are out there somewhere.

"I love Diana so, Marilla. I cannot ever live without her. But I know very well when we grow up that Diana will get married and go away and leave me. And oh, what shall I do? I hate her husband — I just hate him furiously."

Fiction has always explained to me things outside my direct experience. At ten I had people I called friends, but I had yet to meet a "kindred spirit." In Anne's world, kindred spirits are friends between whom there is a meeting of hearts, a strong bond of sympathy, and perfect understanding, regardless of age or gender. The book established an ideal of friendship; it sent me a promise that such friendships could exist.

4. Feminism will save you.

Published in 1908, before full women's suffrage in Canada and decades before the word *feminism* was coined, *Anne of Green*

Gables stands out as an early example of children's literature representing equal rights for women. (Edith Nesbit was also flying the flag around this time in her children's fiction, and earlier novels such as *Jane Eyre* by Charlotte Brontë, 1847, and *Little Women* by Louisa May Alcott, 1868, had criticized gender constraints imposed on women.) In a household where one of my jobs was making my brother's bed, *Anne of Green Gables* was probably my first encounter with feminism.

When Anne and some fellow classmates have the opportunity to sit the entrance exam for Queen's (a teaching academy), Marilla's response to the prospect of further study is:

> *"When Matthew and I took you to bring up we resolved we would do the best we could for you and give you a good education. I believe in a girl being fitted to earn her own living whether she ever has to or not."*

Anne not only aces the entrance exam (Diana cries, *"Anne, you've passed, passed the* very first — *you and Gilbert both — you're ties — but your name is first. Oh, I'm so proud!"*); she also goes on to qualify for the two-year course in one year and wins a scholarship, which will allow her to do a BA at college. What an endorsement for women's higher education and economic independence. And how important for girls of the era to see this narrative played out. More than a hundred years later, Anne's ambitions and triumphs are still a delight to read.

5. Romance doesn't look like that; it looks like this.

> *And then — thwack! Anne had brought her slate down on Gilbert's head and cracked it — slate not head — clear across.*

In the years before I encountered *Anne of Green Gables,* my toys included a teddy bear, dolls, a baby doll, dolls' clothes, doll's cot, doll's pusher . . . I could not have had a more gendered toy selection. Despite evidence to the contrary in the hair-raising fairy tales of Charles Perrault, which I read at age nine, I believed that charming princes played a part in happy endings and that romance-love-marriage-children was a girl-destiny default setting, whatever else I might do. (I didn't have a clue what that would be, though my stock answer at ten was: write and illustrate children's books.)

I've never smashed a slate over anyone's head, but I was attracted to this clear signal that Anne had agency in establishing the terms of her relationship with Gilbert Blythe. She and Gilbert would, over the course of many more books, be depicted as equals in every respect, though, with this decisive *thwack,* Anne held the balance of power for some time.

As well, Anne is portrayed as being unabashedly competitive with Gilbert for academic success, and this is expressed in very positive terms. There's no coming second, or being less ambitious.

There was open rivalry between Gilbert and Anne now. Previously the rivalry had been rather one-sided, but there was no longer any doubt that Gilbert was as determined to be first in class as Anne was. He was a foeman worthy of her steel.

Anne's feistiness was an adrenaline shot, a much-needed antidote to my pink-is-for-girls, sugar-and-spice early indoctrination. When boy time came around, I had snark when I needed it. I also had the representation of a romance between equally matched partners—no rescue by charming prince required. When I finished my Year Twelve exams, I gave myself

the treat of rereading *Anne of the Island*, the volume in which
L. M. Montgomery finally unites Anne and Gilbert.

6. It's not the end of the world if you mess up.

> *"Oh, don't you see, Marilla? There must be a limit to the*
> *mistakes one person can make, and when I get to the end of*
> *them, then I'll be through with them. That's a very comforting*
> *thought."*

Anne frequently acts impulsively, makes mistakes, and
ruefully recognizes her own shortcomings. Losing her temper
and lashing out at Mrs. Lynde; serving currant wine instead
of raspberry cordial to Diana, resulting in being banished as a
suitable companion; taking a dare to walk along the ridge of a
roof and falling off; flavoring a cake with liniment instead of
vanilla; dying her hair green instead of black.

As a child I was shy, self-conscious, and timid, and often felt
foolish: the rules of the world were mysterious to me. I agonized
over saying or doing the wrong thing. It was hugely liberating
to see a character like Anne making large-scale mistakes and
recovering from the grief, injury, or embarrassment that ensued.
Anne was self-reliant and self-directed: she came up with her
own solutions. She forgave herself and was forgiven. And she
could laugh at her mistakes, given a little time for reflection.

7. Read on!

Anne of Green Gables taught me about delayed gratification
as a reader. My first encounter with the first chapter was very
disappointing. It's full of old people! What a relief (a few pages
into chapter 2) to finally meet Anne. This "boring" first chapter

became part of the delight of rereading. I never skipped it. I read it knowing that things were about to get interesting. Not a bad habit to be in, when you think of all the good books that take a bit of time to warm up—*Wuthering Heights* is one that comes to mind.

8. You're not the only unholy girl in the whole world.

I was brought up as a Roman Catholic but never believed in God—not even as a small child. An early memory I have is casting my eyes down and trying to look pious at my first communion ceremony, because I knew it was expected of me.

Perhaps it would have been different if we'd had a more interesting parish priest, but ours was a droning windbag and everything he said had the strong odor of malarkey.

The older character of Anne is certainly depicted as having religious faith. But I was drawn to the early Anne, who had not been a regular churchgoer or Sunday school attendee. It was her careless irreverence that thrilled my faithless heart.

My lack of religious belief was not something I would have dreamed of speaking about, but reading *Anne of Green Gables* gave my undisclosed skepticism some welcome company.

"I never say any prayers," announced Anne. . . . "Mrs. Thomas told me that God made my hair red on purpose, *and I've never cared about Him since. And anyhow, I'd always be too tired at night to bother saying prayers."*

I love beauty.

Becoming Human
Bernard Beckett

Woody Allen once said, with his typically self-pitying brand of humor, that every film he made started out in his head as a piece of art, and then as production began and the first truckload of compromises arrived, step-by-step transformed itself into something shabby and real.

I have to say, I like the image much more than the sentiment.

Compromise, it seems to me, is a thing to be celebrated, not bemoaned. Purity of purpose is for the lunatic who refuses to accept that any work is ever finished, or any effort is ever worthy. It is a kind of self-delusion, based as it is upon the assumption that greatness beckons. For those of us wallowing in the quotidian, compromise is the very stuff of life: the rock from which our greatest moments of creativity are hewn.

You don't need to be a filmmaker or a novelist to recognize this. You only need to bake a cake, plan a party, plant a vegetable garden, or attempt to raise a child to find a kind of beauty in the natural tension that develops between our base impotence and the picture on the tin.

Before I had children, the words I would have most readily associated with parenthood would have been: nurturing, stimulating, bonding, entertaining, interacting — purposeful, virtuous verbs, calling to mind the super-parent, shaping both child and the world around them. Now, with my twin boys almost ready for school, I realize a more apt list would include: distracting, separating, enduring, collapsing, and even, say it quietly, ignoring. Because they're exhausting little blighters, and a person has only so much energy, patience, and spare hands to offer. What's more, if we didn't embrace compromise, think what creatures we would become, and how our children would suffer it. Yes, children need stimulation, but not too much. They need a parent who loves them and wants what is best for them, but not one who is neurotic. They need to be protected, but not hovered over; after all it is only when they are left to make mistakes that they can learn the art of assessing risk. They need to be supported in their education, but not to the point where they feel their parents living vicariously through them. It's not their job to please us. In other words, our commitment to compromise, the need to sometimes just get them the hell out of our hair so that we can get something done, provides exactly the sort of balance the child needs. (The writing of the above paragraph was interrupted by my son calling out from his bed. "I felt something coming in my brain," he told me. "What?" I asked. "Being thirsty." Now he's had his water and has fallen silent again.)

Which brings me, in a roundabout way, to a recent car

journey. We, the family of four, were driving about the countryside in search of a new car: a process that is tedious for an adult, and bafflingly so for a child. Still, needs must and as the kilometers and hours passed by (not just any car, you see; it had to be the right car), the boys grew restless. Super-parent might have responded with a spontaneous sing-along, a diverting game of I Spy, or pulling over to the side of the road for a scrumptious beet and quinoa salad. Compromise-parent fumbled through the CDs in search of something, anything, that might shut them up. Enter, stage left, the inimitable Roald Dahl, and a rather beautiful reading of *George's Marvelous Medicine* (thank you, June Whitfield). Now, our boys are well used to distractions of this nature. Even at their tender years, they have a deep appreciation of the classics (*Toy Story, Shrek, Fantastic Mr. Fox, WALL-E,* you know of what I speak). Up until that point of the road trip, I had seen them sit entranced as these movie-stories had unfolded. I had heard them gasp, laugh and shout, and sing along as the masters of children's cinema had woven their magic. But never, I swear, had I heard them laugh in the way they laughed at that story. It was a kind of out-of-control, infectious giggling that took hold of them, and I glanced in my rearview mirror to witness each turned in his car seat, eyeballing the other, feeding off the reaction. And that moment reminded me of something that I, as a writer, should never have needed reminding of. That storytelling in its purest form — some words, a voice — is compelling in a way that no other medium can be.

Who was it who said that "literature is the only art form in which the audience provides the score"? I don't remember, and Google is being unhelpful. Never mind, the point is an important one. When we read a story, or indeed listen to one, the only way to comprehend it is to fully engage with it. The words must become alive inside our heads, sounds that denote nothing more than symbols become chickens, grandmothers, and explosions. And it is the work being done by the reader, a process so oblique that any attempt to deconstruct it seems doomed to failure, that ensures a relationship between the work and the audience that is closer and more committed than it is in any other art. We own the story because we are, to such a large extent, creating it. (Theater, I must concede, has its own claim to emotional primacy. The palpable presence of the flesh-and-blood characters before us creates its own sort of magic.) To look back at my boys and see the intensity of their connection with the text was to experience the magic of story in a way that I, as an adult, had all but forgotten.

Children, of course, have a capacity to commit to imaginary worlds that adults struggle to match. Many days my boys appear to spend more time in roles than out of them. Not the subtle versions of ourselves we self-consciously present to the world, but full-scale transformations to ballerina, superhero, train driver, or marine biologist. They cope with these nested identities without a blink: "No, I am Sebastian being Gold Boy pretending to be Freeze, but really I am in disguise as Bat Boy." There is something weirdly compelling about that fantastical living, and I feel more than the odd pang of jealousy when I see it. To watch a child succumb to a story is to be reminded of the magic that resides in a world still protean and malleable. In part it explains the depth of my joy when I heard them laughing.

Still, there are layers to my response to my boys' reaction to June Whitfield's reading of Roald Dahl's story, to continue with the nesting theme. There is a part of me that refuses to let go of the idea that the very habit of storytelling, and story receiving, is of itself virtuous. There is undoubtedly a little bit of prejudice and nostalgia in play here, but I think it goes deeper than that. Not only does story demand that we imagine whole worlds into existence, but it forces us to imagine something much more specific: the existence, and motives, of other people. It is through story, be it a novel or a good gossip with a friend, that we develop and refine our theory of mind. We go looking for the perspective that resides in another's head. And by trying on for a moment their fears, their desires, their habits, and their constraints, we become more human, more empathetic. Remarkably, the human brain, when observing or indeed imagining the experiences of others, brings into play the exact structures that fire when it is having the same experience itself. This, for my money, even more than language or sense of self, is the quality that defines and, by implication, raises us. To see your children become lost in a story is to watch them exercise their most sacred capacity. And that's true even when the story itself is so gleefully brutal.

This is the part where I confess the real reason I was so delighted by the youngsters' reaction to the story. I was delighting in the story too. Like them, I had never come across it before. And so to enjoy it for the first time in the company of my children was particularly fine. And enjoy it I did. Because Dahl is a master of the revolting and the unspeakable. I remember as a child being read to from a great tome of tales from the Brothers Grimm. We angst in our modern times over what does and doesn't constitute appropriate fare for the young, and I still recall how confronting Hansel and Gretel's abandonment was. But I dealt with it, and by the end of the tale the old woman had been murdered, the evil stepmother sent away, and all was well. Our instinct is to keep our children safe from horror, and from humor that might hint at any kind of viciousness, but again, there is beauty to be uncovered when our ideals are compromised. In *George's Marvelous Medicine,* there is no politeness offered. Grandma may be the family's elder, but she is afforded no respect. Rather, she is described in the opening passages as selfish and grumpy, and her puckered mouth is compared to a dog's bottom.

How we children laughed.

To be clear, this is not a tale where enemies learn, in time, to begrudgingly respect one another. George does not learn of his grandma's kinder side, or discover the pains in her past that have made her the way she is. Nor does some act of selflessness from the boy teach the woman to respect him. Rather, George attempts to poison the old dear, and when this is only partially successful, his father conspires to help her take too much of the antidote, to the point where she doesn't so much die as shrink out of existence.

At this point her own daughter, rather than express any regret at her passing, concedes she was something of a nuisance to have around the house.

The transgressive nature of the best children's literature, its ability to celebrate out loud that which cannot be thought in public, is a thing to be savored. As is the view in the rearview mirror of two delightful boys, lost in story, cackling together, becoming human.

I seek truth.

Looking Where I'm Standing
Felicity Castagna

S andra Cisneros taught me that the parking lot in the image below is something extraordinary, and that idea made me a better writer and a better human being.

Cisneros's book *The House on Mango Street* (1984) is the story of a Latina girl named Esperanza Cordero who spends her time living in too many different places as a child until her family of six finally buys a small house on Mango Street in a friendly but often rough neighborhood of Chicago. This young adult novel is told in vignette form—a kind of short, short story that uses highly poetic imagery to focus on a small place and moment in time. The book uses the vignette style to take us from a little house and out into the streets, where small things are examined and their larger significance unraveled: the peeling red paint of a too-small house, the swaying hips of women as they strut down the street, the bike all the neighborhood children take turns riding, the woman who stares out the window of her house because her husband thinks she is too beautiful to be let out, the tired-looking men who hang out with each other on street corners.

It's a book about a lot of things, but to me it is most importantly a book about place, about community and the importance of thinking deeply about where you are standing. Somehow this book has always managed to show up in my life whenever I needed it. When I first read this book in my Year Nine English class, I *was* Esperanza—an awkward, lonely girl whose family had moved so many times, across state and national borders, and all I wanted in life was my own "house on Mango Street" where I could have a place to be for a while. In my twenties, the book came back again several times, always at the right time, following me around by showing up in garage sales, the bookshelves at strangers' parties, and once, I kid you not, beside me on a train. And still now I dip in and out of its pages every time I get too busy or too distracted and forget to notice what's going on around me.

My first young adult novel, *The Incredible Here and Now*, emerged out of so many years of thinking about *The House on*

Mango Street, not just about what I could learn from it as a writer, but for what it taught me about the importance of observing the everydayness of the place you live in. Good writing about place comes from this observation of detail; from extracting the extraordinariness out of these ordinary things, like empty parking lots, that we see every day but sometimes fail to really notice. It presents us with more than just images—it gives us an invitation to experience the world we know in an entirely different way.

Working out how to belong in a place and how to write about it are for me very similar things. A sense of place applies most powerfully to the most commonplace and unremarkable things: the Pontiac that speeds down my street on weekdays at lunchtime, the vending machines in front of the Coke factory on my way to work, the Coles trolleys left by the river, the look of George's rough hands as he bags my groceries at the corner store. Being from somewhere is about gathering these images, connecting memory to imagination, using these fragments to construct your own story of place.

Sometimes it's really hard to remember to look at the place where you are standing. You can tell when you read *The House on Mango Street* that Cisneros has spent a lot of time walking, imagining, thinking. Writing about place is an expression of what is specific and local, but it is also an expression of how we imagine the world that we live in. This is what I try to remember when I am writing about the western suburbs of Sydney: that when we write about places that are important to us, we can change the way that outsiders imagine it. Change the imagination and you can change the world.

But what does this have to do with images of parking lots?

Parking lots are where life happens when you're not thinking about it very much. So are backyards and side streets and apartment balconies. If you can't find the extraordinariness that exists in these ordinary spaces, you can't be a writer. You can miss all these things because you're not noticing, thinking, imagining. Being in the moment, being exactly where you are and looking at that giant arrow that points off into nowhere, that's when you make those connections between story and life and life back to story. *The House on Mango Street* is a book that makes me look at where I'm standing over and over again and inspires me to write about it.

This World Is More Than What Can Be Seen
Ambelin Kwaymullina

They've asked me to write about the book that made me. Only I can't, because the story that made me, the one that flows through my mind and heart and veins, isn't in a book. It's a lot older than that. Older than the invention of the printing press, older even than the stone tablets of the Romans or the papyrus scrolls of the Egyptians. It is the tale of an ancient people in an ancient land.

The story of Aboriginal people in Australia begins in the Dreaming, when the creative Ancestors made the world and everything that exists within it now. The Ancestors came in different forms — rock and crow and dingo, the seven sisters who became stars, and many, many others. They shaped the different Aboriginal homelands of Australia, the places that we call our

Countries, and they taught us how to sustain a living land. It is their stories that make all stories possible.

The Country of my people, the Palyku, lies in the Pilbara region of Western Australia. The Pilbara is a place of far horizons and vivid contrasting colors—red earth, purple hills, green gum trees, and long blue skies. Like all Aboriginal Countries, my homeland is rich in story. The great libraries of the Aboriginal nations of this continent are not built of bricks or steel. Our knowledge is written into the land and our old people highly literate in reading the earth around them. But when strangers arrived on these shores, they did not understand our ways of knowing. And the arrival of the colonizers marked the beginning of another set of tales, the stories of the generations of Aboriginal people who lived the trauma of colonialism.

These tales, too, are part of the story that makes me, and they are tales of terror, of violence and heartbreak. But they also tell of courage, of defiance, and of endurance against all odds and in the face of determined efforts to destroy. So many of those who survived what were among the worst of times, the men and women of my great-grandmothers' generation, are people of boundless generosity of spirit. Their tales speak of what is perhaps the last choice anyone has left when all other options are stripped away—the choice to be better than the times in which you live or the way in which you are treated. And it is their incredible strength that makes possible the stories of all who came after.

The tale of who I am is formed by, and linked with, so many others. The Dreaming Ancestors created a reality where everything lives and everything connects in an ever-moving network of relationships. This world is more than what can be seen, perhaps even than what can be felt, and in such a place, it is wise to be respectful of the life around you. Everything has a story, and it is impossible to determine the millions of ways in which the tales of the different shapes of life who inhabit this earth intersect with our own. I worry about the species who are struggling to survive. What will my story become without the ancient wisdom of a Loggerhead Turtle, the fierceness of a Chuditch (quoll), or the gentleness of a Pilbara Olive Python? We humans cannot see far enough to grasp the extent to which we are all diminished by the loss of stories from this earth.

Aboriginal stories are found in many places. In Country, in our hearts, in song and art and dance. And in books, some of which are written in the ancient languages of this land. We are many voices, and I am proud to be among the Aboriginal storytellers of Australia. The stories I create are for children and teenagers, and much of what I write is about the future. It seems to me that the world can often be an unjust place, and those injustices impact most terribly on the young. Perhaps because of this, I am obsessed with the tale of what could be, with the possibility of a place where all stories are valued. I glimpse this future, sometimes. I see it in dreams, in books, and most of all in the actions of good-hearted people across the globe who do what they can to bring positive change to this planet.

I want everyone who will come after me to inherit an earth bursting with diversity—of species, of voices, of cultures, of ideas. And I know that the future is a story to which we all contribute. So look. Look ahead. What do you want to see happen? Will you let the world shape you, or will you shape the world? I know it can be hard, especially when choices are few and obstacles are many. But your life, your choices, your dreams — they matter. We can none of us know the extent to which our story will intersect with the stories of others. Find your path, and let no one diminish it, or you.

Every story matters, and we all have the power to influence the future.

I can live many lives.

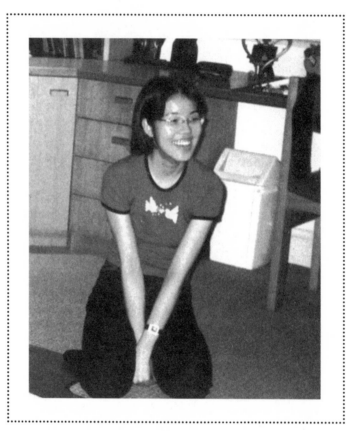

What the Doctor Recommended
Queenie Chan

In order to talk about the book that made me, I must first talk about my cousin Munn.

If Munn was not quite the person who made me, then he was the person who gave me the tools to shape myself into who I am today.

Many books that change lives often come with two people attached — the one who wrote the book and the one who pressed that book into your hand, urging you to read it. Cousin Munn was one of the latter, and he had caught me at that most formative time of my life — when I was a young teenager.

By day, Doctor Munn is a mild-mannered emergency room (ER) doctor working at Queen Mary Hospital, in Pok Fu Lam, Hong Kong. By night, he is a wellspring of information on manga, anime, and video games. He's the type of guy who is always "in the know." He knows all about the latest popular trends, and whatever he's into at the moment, he will sell it to you like he's a guru pitching spiritual enlightenment.

(He's actually a really good salesman. Looks like the world gained a good doctor but lost a potential cult leader.)

I was born in Hong Kong, in 1980. For the first few years of my life, I was reared on manga and anime, the Japanese terms for comics and cartoons. When I migrated to Australia in 1986, I lost touch with Doraemon, Urusei Yatsura, and countless other manga, until my family started taking yearly trips back to Hong Kong. This started when I was ten years old, and it continues to this day.

On some of these trips, Cousin Munn would meet us at the airport, to take the kids out shopping for the latest cartoon books. This was in the mid-1990s, and he would take us to massive four-story shopping centers in Mong Kok, where *every. single. shop.* sold either manga, anime, or video games.

TO ME, THIS WAS COOL CENTRAL.

COUSIN MUNN WOULD THEN SWEEP THE SHELVES,

BUYING ME THE LATEST POPULAR MANGA IN THE NAME OF "CULTURAL EDUCATION."

(The adults, meanwhile, would gratefully check into the nearest hotel, eager to sleep off the jet lag. We would return from our shopping trip, and my parents would wake to find the hotel room wall to wall with all my new manga and video game purchases.)

As an overly serious ten-year-old, I looked up to Cousin Munn (*the man!*) as an arbiter of good taste. I knew that whenever he pointed his finger at anything pop-culture related, there was bound to be something fun and interesting in that direction.

ONE DAY,

HE HANDED ME A MANGA ABOUT A DOCTOR.

Not a mad scientist, not Doctor Who, but a *medical* doctor.

A *surgeon,* in fact. The surgeon's name was Black Jack, which was, not coincidentally, also the name of the manga series.

Well, it's no surprise that a doctor would recommend a manga about a doctor; people love seeing themselves reflected in fiction. However, my own interests sat squarely in fantasy: knights, wizards, and demon kings battling it out in epic battles of good and evil. I was around fifteen at the time, and in the Queenie-verse, manga was only ever about two things: swords-and-sorcery fantasy realms, or high-school romances (with or without vampires).

I pretended I was happy and interested in Black Jack, but really, I wasn't. I knew what kind of art and stories I liked, and this was neither. The art, especially, was *weird*. It was old-school cartoony and unappealing, and Black Jack himself looked like a cross between Cruella de Vil and Dracula. Of course, Cousin Munn must have sensed this, because he rolled out his famous sales pitch.

According to him:

BLACK JACK IS A RIVETING TALE ABOUT A ROGUE SURGEON,

A MEDICAL MAVERICK WHOSE TALENTS ARE HIGHLY SOUGHT AFTER.

HE'S A GENIUS IN HIS FIELD BUT UNLICENSED,

BECAUSE HE WOULD CHARGE HIS CLIENTS EXORBITANT FEES, WHICH IS WELL, UNETHICAL.

BLACK JACK IS ABOUT THIS MAN AND HIS SHADOWY PAST,

BUT ALSO HIS PATIENTS, AND THE STRANGE REAL-LIFE ILLNESSES THEY HAVE TO DEAL WITH.

For a brief moment, life returned to my eyes. I recalled the brave little boy robot with rockets for legs, horns for hair, and a machine gun for a butt. I had religiously watched the Saturday-morning cartoon as a kid in Sydney, and even fifteen-year-olds are capable of feeling nostalgia.

I gave Cousin Munn a huge smile, thanked him, and then shoved Black Jack right to the bottom of my reading pile.

Needless to say, I then went right back to the hotel and plowed through all my new action-adventure and swords-and-sorcery manga.

My favorite manga were Dragon Ball Z and Dragon Quest at that time (I was *obsessed*), and my mind was preoccupied with high-stakes midair battles between warriors blasting each other with huge energy balls. There was no room left in my mind for a quiet story about an unethical surgeon. Not even one who will undoubtedly turn out to have a heart of gold and a core of inner strength.

As anyone who's ever read manga will know, you can easily get through ten volumes of manga in a little under four hours. That was exactly what happened, when I found myself staring at the last book in my pile.

WELL, HELLO, DOCTOR!

IT WOULD BE A HUGE CLICHÉ TO SAY THAT THIS BOOK "CHANGED MY LIFE."

IT'S PROBABLY MORE APPROPRIATE TO SAY THAT THIS BOOK "OPENED A DOOR."

The crucial lesson I learned from reading Black Jack is that a good storyteller can make *any* story interesting.

Black Jack was a series of short stories with recurring characters, and Munn was right when he called it *riveting*. There were no

formulas in the world of Black Jack, or at least none I could easily predict. The endings were not always happy, and the patients Black Jack cured sometimes didn't really want to be cured.

In short, these were stories about humanity. People who behaved in unpredictable ways, as people often do, for reasons they sometimes don't fully understand themselves.

Some of them were honorable and some of them were weak, but all of them had

reasons I could comprehend and even feel sympathetic toward.

Reading those stories in that little hotel room, it made me realize the limitations of doctors—what they ultimately can do and cannot do. I used to believe that doctors were "lifesavers," angels who swooped in to rescue people on the brink of death, but it turned out to be more complicated than that. Truth is, sometimes people didn't want to be saved, and sometimes they *couldn't* be saved—even from themselves. Doctors can't force their patients to see things differently. They can only take the lead, pointing in the right direction and hoping their patients will see things their way.

Among the other things Black Jack blew to smithereens was my belief that all manga is fantasy or high-school romance. Heck, that was *miles* away from the truth—a good manga can be about anything under the sun. It's a medium, not a genre, and if a story about a surgeon can be interesting, so can a story about a firefighter (Megumi no Daigo, for example).

Years later, when I became a professional manga artist, I would always remember the valuable lesson of Black Jack. Not just that I was now on the other side of that door, producing books that knocked on the doors of readers—but that I was once a reluctant reader myself.

So many things can seem dull at first glance. So many things can make you roll your eyes, and think . . . *Really?!* So many things can turn someone away from cracking open a new book, and most of all, the people whose job it is to introduce books to others can sometimes give the wrong sales pitch. However, given the right pathways, the right person, and the right alignment of the stars, a book can send someone down a completely different life path from the one they were on before.

Believe it or not, I had originally graduated from university with a degree in Information Systems, but I bypassed that career path to become a manga artist. In 2004, two years after I graduated, I wrote and illustrated my first published manga, a mystery-horror story called *The Dreaming*. It was an amazing experience, and I haven't looked back since.

I want to experience emotion.

Of Magic and Memory
Kate Constable

The bookish child sits in a quiet corner of a suburban house, turning pages. Inside her imagination, she's a million miles away: exploring jungles, sailing distant seas, having swashbuckling adventures in wild and distant lands.

I was the other way around.

My home was in the middle of a wild and perilous country, a mysterious land of thick jungles, impenetrable mountain ranges, crashing thunderstorms, and unpredictable earthquakes. The small town where I lived was situated among remote valleys, discovered by the outside world only a few decades earlier, a place of breathtaking natural beauty and violent warfare between spear-wielding warriors. But while the thunderstorms raged, I was snug in a corner of our little fibrocement house, reading.

And what I read were books set in the sedate English countryside, stories written years before I was born, safely distant in both time and place from the confusing reality outside my door.

I spent most of my childhood in Papua New Guinea, in the Highlands town of Mount Hagen. Back in the 1970s, Hagen was a frontier town, a colonial outpost.

Once a week, on market day, local men from the villages would stalk into town, traditionally dressed with cloth *laplaps* hanging from their belts in front and *as-gras* like a bustle of leaves behind, sporting grand headdresses of fur and feathers, and necklaces of shells. Their wives followed behind, bowed down under the weight of the laden string *bilum* bags that hung off their foreheads. My mum would stock up on the fresh fruit and vegetables they carried, grown in the villages and hillside gardens surrounding the town, and I would stock up on books at the small but excellent library, located just next to the market.

There wasn't much else to do in Mount Hagen but read. No television, hardly any shops, no swimming pools or playgrounds. We'd listen to my dad's LPs of British comedy shows like *The Goon Show* and *Hancock's Half Hour* until we could recite them word for word. When we came back to Australia, I knew nothing about football or fashion or pop music. I might as well have landed from another planet.

My world was books. I've tried to find out more about the Mount Hagen public library, without success; it doesn't seem to exist anymore. But I suspect now that the well-stocked children's section, at least, might have been shipped to the Highlands all of a piece, as a government initiative or a charitable impulse by someone. It had *The Railway Children* and the Bastable series, *Little Women* and *Little House on the Prairie*, the Narnia books and *The Little White Horse,* the Dido Twite books and *A Wrinkle in Time, The Children of Green Knowe* and *The Borrowers,* ballet books and pony books. I gulped them all down. I borrowed my favorite books over and over, sometimes not even bothering to open them; I'd sleep with them under my pillow so they'd enter my dreams. Some particular favorites were part of a process I called "dreaming about": imagining myself as part of their story, in the hazy time just before falling asleep. *The Summer of the Great Secret,* a solidly written but fairly unadventurous pony book by Monica Edwards, set in the Romney Marshes, for some reason captured my imagination utterly for about two years.

One of the books I returned to over and over, not because I dreamed myself into it, but because I loved it with a deeper love, was *Tom's Midnight Garden.*

Written in 1958, it's the story of Tom, exiled to his childless aunt and uncle's apartment for the holidays because of his twin brother's measles. When he arrives, he's disappointed to find that their flat, part of a large old house, has no garden. But lying awake one night, he hears the grandfather clock in the hallway strike thirteen, and when Tom wanders downstairs, he discovers that he has entered the house's past.

When he opens the back door, he finds not the small yard with rubbish bins that exists in the daytime, but the original huge garden that once belonged to the house before its grounds were sold off. Exploring the garden, he finds that he is a "ghost" in this time; none of the inhabitants of the house are aware of him—none except Hatty, the young orphan girl adopted by the rather cold, cruel family of the house.

Lonely Hatty and lonely Tom become friends. Together they climb trees, make a bow and arrows, and explore the nearby river and fields. Tom encourages Hatty to take risks, and Hatty falls out of a tree and is almost killed, and Tom realizes that she is growing older much faster than he is.

In the garden it's always high summer, until one night Tom enters the garden and finds that winter has come. He and Hatty skate together down the frozen river as darkness falls, and at last Hatty is given a lift home by a neighbor, seeming to ignore Tom completely. He is outraged by this betrayal, and the next night, the last of his stay, he finds he can't enter the garden. It's gone, and he blunders into the rubbish bins of the present-day yard, calling desperately for Hatty.

This commotion wakes everyone in the house, and this is how he discovers that Hatty is, in fact, old Mrs. Bartholomew. She is the owner of the house, the shadowy inhabitant of the topmost flat, and she has been dreaming of her childhood, night after night, summoning the garden, and Tom himself, into her dreams. On Tom's final day, the two friends are joyously reunited.

The last scene has always stayed with me: Tom is about to go home, but having bid a polite farewell to old Mrs. Bartholomew, he impulsively turns and rushes back up the stairs to hug her, as if she were his own age and they'd been friends all their lives.

Tom's Midnight Garden is not a fast-paced book; it's slow and atmospheric, every detail of the garden lovingly described (I wasn't surprised to learn that the house and garden in the book were based on Philippa Pearce's childhood home), and Tom and Hatty's adventures are leisurely and largely undramatic. But it was a book I felt I could live inside, as if time stopped while I was within its pages. And for me, the simple elegance of the central time slip has never been surpassed. The final scenes, when Tom discovers that the wrinkled old lady upstairs and the lively young companion of his midnight garden are one and the same, are so poignant and so deeply satisfying.

I recently read this book aloud to my daughter, and she foresaw the "twist" long before I had on first reading, but for me, the joy of the twist was going back to reread and pick up all the clues to Hatty's real identity.

When I was ten, *Tom's Midnight Garden* gave me ideas I didn't understand, ideas to mull over. What was dream, and what was reality? Who was the ghost, Hatty or Tom? Did Tom create Hatty's memories, or did Hatty build a reality for Tom to enter? Tom puzzles over the nature of time itself, its shape and form: Does it fly ever forward like an arrow or a river, or loop back on itself, repeating its patterns like the seasons of a garden? Can two realities exist at once? It was my first real introduction to the mysteries of "timey-wimeyness."

Children's books are the right place to explore big ideas, philosophical truths, and ruminations on the world, before adolescence hits and it all becomes about personal journeys, when one's own mysterious self is the most fascinating object in the universe. About twelve is the age when a young person best grapples with these big thoughts, old enough to grasp their implications, young enough for the ideas to be startling and fresh.

Something that had entered deep into my unconscious, without my knowing it, were the chapters where Hatty and Tom skate down the frozen river, night falling around them. These beautiful, haunting scenes resurfaced in my own writing in the icebound scenes of my book *The Tenth Power*, but it wasn't until I reread *Tom's Midnight Garden* that I recognized, with a jolt, their true origin.

At around the age of eleven or twelve, time-slip stories held a particular magic for me. I was bewitched by Alison Uttley's *A Traveler in Time*, fascinated but unsettled by *Charlotte Sometimes* by Penelope Farmer, and enchanted by Joan G. Robinson's *When*

Marnie Was There. Penelope Lively's *The Ghost of Thomas Kempe*, with its similar reflections on time and memory, also captured my imagination.

I dreamed of entering other times, other worlds. Perhaps, living in untamed, dangerous colonial Papua New Guinea, I unconsciously sought security in the pages of my best-loved books, worlds of magic and memory, an imagined England that no longer existed in reality, if it ever had. But ultimately, when we open a book, aren't we all trying to enter our own secret midnight garden?

I like the words.
I like the pictures.

The Big Scooby-Doo Reveal
Rachael Craw

A scrawny ten-year-old girl, all elbows and knees, face plastered with freckles, scratching at her nape beneath a short sandy wig of tatty curls—that was me on Book Day at Kendal Primary School, Standard Four. Fossicked from the dusty innards of my mother's wardrobe, that wig was a relic from the sixties and a boon for an otherwise uninspiring costume of jeans turned up at the ankle and a plain cream shirt. It made my scalp and ears itch and the back of my neck red and sweaty. I wore it the whole day even though it was irritating and the color, like the cream shirt, did nothing for my complexion. It was an act of devotion to my fictional heroine, Trixie Belden.

Trixie came into my life at a time when I needed her most, a tediously rainy school holiday on the West Coast of the South Island of New Zealand, infamous for sand flies and precipitation.

I must have been driving my parents mad with a constant liturgy of "I'm boooored" and "There's nothing to dooooo" and sighing and moaning and making life miserable for everyone in the way that children do when they're trapped indoors by bad weather and a waning appetite for imaginary play.

A mercy dash with my dad to the bookstore, and there I found her—a fascinating thirteen-year-old rural American super-sleuth, resident of fictional Sleepyside-on-Hudson in upstate New York, club member of the Bob-Whites of the Glen, and best friend of wealthy and refined Honey Wheeler. Imagine my thrill upon discovering an entire shelf of adventures to pick from. Though the store didn't have them all, I was eager enough that I didn't even mind diving in midseries. My choice was based on the sheer power of alliteration, a title so exotic and dangerous sounding I could not resist: *The Mystery of the Midnight Marauder*.

Now, I had no clue what a marauder was. I hoped and feared it meant murderer, though I was squeamish of anything blood-thirsty. I had only recently overcome a paralyzing fear of vam-pires after copping an eyeful of the boy next door's graphic encyclopedia of bloodsuckers. Flipping through those dark pages, it was the image of Nosferatu hanging in a bell tower eating him-self from the feet up that burned its way into my synapses. So I was in no hurry to read anything that involved a lot of blood, but the sense of high-stakes mystery that surrounded the word *marauder* drew me in. When I brought the book to the counter for Dad to pay, I made a point of looking as nonchalant as possible. I wasn't idiot enough to ask him outright what the word meant. That would only draw attention to the potentially dangerous subject matter and risk confiscation. No, I played it cool.

Of course, I started the book in the car, and when we got back to my nanna's house I went straight to my room, lay on my bed, and kept reading. By late afternoon I had gotten to know Trixie and her friends: sweet and gentle Honey, the enviably violet-eyed Diana, and big, handsome red-haired Jim. Trixie was sweet on Jim. He gave her an identification bracelet. I suspected that was jewelry and it seemed a promising sign. I don't think I'd ever read anything romantic before. I had started the book amped for mystery and discovered a bonus prize. Occasional flustered blushes, loggerheads arguments, and lingering looks between Trixie and Jim made for giddy plot drivers that kept me turning the pages. Though, disappointingly, I never read a Trixie Belden story where they actually kissed.

Before the day was out, I had learned that a marauder was a roaming thief but that not all thieves were scoundrels. The moral lesson! Trixie, I discovered after several books, was often the beneficiary of the moral lesson, throwing herself into each mystery with righteous certainty, to later trip on her own assumptions. Not all rich people were snobs, not all elderly recluses were hiding terrible secrets in their mansion attics, and not all ethnically diverse people wearing leather jackets were villains. City life, drugs, and motorcycles, however, were invariably bad. The reader might absorb these invaluable truths along with Trixie, usually just in time for the big Scooby-Doo reveal at the end, when culprits were unmasked and motivations explained. *The Mystery of the Midnight Marauder* had all of these features and it ignited my imagination, leaving me hungry for more. Luckily, the rain persisted for several days, and my father, for the sake of his wallet, signed me up at the Greymouth Public Library.

In retrospect, it's fun to try to figure out why these books had so much appeal for me. As an adult I've had no interest in reading crime fiction or mystery novels, though in some respects my own novels in the Spark series carry a thread of mystery through them. I think what ultimately drew me to Trixie Belden stories was Trixie herself, a powerful female protagonist. She wasn't perfect, she had fears and insecurities, and she often made mistakes, but she was an instigator, an investigator, curious, bold, and risk taking. She was a thinker and problem solver who came up with wild theories, a leader in the search for truth. In my later reading, Anne of Green Gables would also attract my attention for being a powerful female protagonist. She expressed herself, her curiosity, her creativity. She questioned authority and was ambitious and competitive, but before I met Anne, Trixie was the business.

I wouldn't have been able to articulate it then, but now I think I was looking for a protagonist I could identify with. I loved that she was outspoken, opinionated, and take-charge. I loved that she had freckles! A shared affliction. It made up for her being more on the blond side of sandy haired. Growing up, I resented the lack of black-haired, pale-skinned heroines in books and on television. There was Wonder Woman, whom I worshipped, but even she had a tan. I wasn't fussed with Snow White, who really just did a lot of housework, fell unconscious, and then married the first man who kissed her. Besides which, she was preternaturally beautiful and I was an ugly child. Or, at least, I felt ugly. I was too tall, too skinny, too pale, too freckly, too loud, and my ears stuck out. The only feature that I loved about myself was my long black hair, but my mother, sick of maintaining it, took me to the hairdresser and had it chopped off! Not into a pretty bob like you might find on little girls today, but short like a boy's. I cried all the way home from the salon.

When I found Trixie, she had short hair, too, admittedly with curls, but freckles and short hair were two more likenesses than I had managed to find anywhere else.

Another big part of the allure of these stories was the potent American-ness of Trixie's life. She and her friends rode a yellow bus to school, where the corridors were lined with metal lockers and the desks were scalloped around the sides of their chairs, where they pledged allegiance to a flag before class began. They carried their lunches in brown paper bags, and they went to pep rallies where cheerleaders turned flips and waved pom-poms. They came home and did chores. Chores! They celebrated Halloween, Thanksgiving, and Fourth of July with corn dogs and pumpkin pies.

I already had a firm scaffold of popular American culture constructed in my psyche thanks to television the likes of *Little House on the Prairie*, *The Dukes of Hazzard*, and *Happy Days* (see Google and YouTube). The Steven Spielberg movie *E.T. the Extra-Terrestrial* had come out when I was eight years old, and, quite apart from the thrill of alien encounter, the scene in the breakfast booth where the kids sat and ate pepperoni pizza straight from the box impacted the wiring of my brain to such an extent that I have never, ever forgotten it. I couldn't get enough of the home of the brave and the land of the free.

Trixie Belden provided that portal to another place, another culture that seemed different, larger, and more interesting than my own. I was young; I hadn't yet fallen in love with the culture or beauty of the landscape in which I lived, though that would come in time. At the age of ten, I felt my home was boring, small, and tedious with its sameness. America was a distant wonderland, glittering with otherness. Thankfully, there were many books in the series, which meant I could return to that wonderland again and again, revisiting those characters like old friends.

That joy I found in reading serial fiction is one of the reasons I wanted to write a series myself, to create a world and characters readers would want to come back to. Trixie also inspired me, along with other strong female protagonists in fiction, to create Evie: a thinker, a planner, an initiator. One who questions authority, reacts to injustice, and goes after the truth. She struggles with her lot, her insecurities and fears, but still takes action. Admittedly, I did allow myself one small indulgence I hope you will forgive me for. I gave her long black hair, pale skin, and freckles.

* I love language.

Sweet Dreams and Social Fails
Simmone Howell

It's 1982. I'm in Grade Five. My teacher is Ms. Babitz.* I have short hair, and my favorite item of clothing is an aqua-blue jumper with piano key sleeves and the words *Rock 'n' roll* repeated over a profusion of musical notes. I go to a public primary school, but for religious education I have to go to the Catholic class and read boring Bible stories while everyone else gets to slack off with the *Sing Sing Sing* book. Lately, I am obsessed with changing. I am a BMX-riding tomboy who aspires to glamour. Sadly, my eyes are too big and my nose is too big and my body is lumpy. I have two best friends who look great in stretch Fabergé jeans. Also, they have perms. In the past year, I have used my pocket money to binge on Cadbury Snack and Fry's Turkish delight; I have tasted Cinzano and added water to cover up the sneak; I have fashioned a bra from a pair of my mum's stockings and rubber bands; I record the name of every movie I watch on a big sheet of paper on the back of my door. Ours is a bookish household, and for the most part I read what I'm given, but all of this is about to change. Because I have discovered Sweet Dreams books.

I spend my pocket money on them. I read them while walking. They are not brilliant works of literature. They are not classics. They are challenging only in that they force me to look at my life and acknowledge how very wrong it is. I gravitate toward the ones that have dark-haired cover girls, but I never pretend that the girl is me — our differences are too huge. For one thing, she's in America; for another, she usually has two boys to choose from. She may have another interest — photography or art or dancing — but it's never BMX, so I don't even get that right. I am not looking for myself in these books; I'm looking for the person *I could become*. The books are short enough to read in a single sitting and full of social arcana. I think they might be Key. Already I have learned that boys don't like it if you're too loud, or pushy, or if you make the first move. I know that competition between girls is fierce, but for even the dorkiest of dorkgirls, love may be just a daring shade of eye shadow away.

Annie, of *Ask Annie* (Sweet Dreams #17), has spent her summer riding her bike to the local pool to swim laps, then coming home to carrot sticks. Now that she's metamorphosed into the kind of girl who looks cute even in a pair of white overalls, she needs to work on her personality. The problem is simple: Annie is awkward around boys. How to deal? Annie deals by taking on the role of agony aunt, but when her crush (Tim) keeps hounding her about how to handle his girlfriend, Annie has to work out how she can help herself. From *Ask Annie* I learn that if you ride your bike to the pool every day and swim laps over the summer, you will become "svelte." I also learn the word *egocentric*. (I think it was from *Ask Annie*, but it might have been from *Green Eyes* [Sweet Dreams #7] or *The Trouble with Charlie* [Sweet Dreams #24]. I can't pretend the books haven't blurred somewhat over time.)

This social disorder of being unable to talk to boys is a big one. I collect appropriate behaviors from Sweet Dreams books, but I can't seem to demonstrate them. I express my affection for Carl Harrison by way of a physical fight on the roof of my primary school. I take Mark Berringer's glasses and hold them above his head until his eyes start leaking. I tell Andre Popova that he has nice knees. Time and again Romance fails to ensue.

In *The Popularity Plan* (Sweet Dreams #2) shy girl Frannie has a cute best friend (Charlene) who sets Frannie certain challenges that force her to interact with boys—such as the ol' rolling your pencil under his desk technique and phoning him up with a list of talking points in hand. It seems like Charlene's plan is working—Frannie has many dates with many boys, but it's the shy guy in her art class that she really likes (Ronnie), and the more popular she appears, the more he stays in the background. Eventually, though, Frannie and Ronnie find their way—as all perfect couples do. *The Popularity Plan* is followed by *The Popularity Summer* (Sweet Dreams #20), where Frannie—now cured—stays with her shy cousin Joleen and teaches her everything she knows. If Joleen's ever going to get a boyfriend, she first needs to get a tan—Joleen is described as having skin like the underside of a fish, a simile that I have carried with me ever since (and possibly appropriated).

To twelve-year-old me, the idea that the subject of boys can be taught like maths (or math, as our American friends call it) is exciting but not exacting. And despite my failures, I persist. By now my affection is somewhat split between Sweet Dreams books (which are stand-alones but thematically linked) and my first experience of series romance, Sweet Valley High. Every time I go to the bookshop, there's a new one out. I am obsessed with the Wakefield twins, Jessica and Elizabeth of the five feet six and matching golden lavaliere necklaces. Elizabeth is good. Jessica is bad. Of course I like Jessica. I appreciate the way she wields lip liner and conjugates her French verbs. ("Bore, Bored, Boring.") Elizabeth is such a square. Sweet Valley High, while still fluffy, is racier than Sweet Dreams books. The world is populated with the kind of stereotypes that dwell in first drafts: the rich cad, the snobby society princess, the long-suffering nerd, the girl from the wrong side of the tracks, the conniving best friend, the class clown. Sweet Valley High also introduces me to rapists, drug addicts, stalkers, and PTSD. It's a black-armband day when Regina Morrow snorts cocaine and dies at Molly Hecht's party (*On the Edge*, Sweet Valley High #40). Vale.

But this is what happens: without my noticing, the field expands. The world is full of stuff, and SVH is like the gateway to everything, everything, EVERYTHING!

Flowers in the Attic is doing the rounds. A babysitter shows us *Puberty Blues*. At a slumber party we watch *Sleepaway Camp;* the film's twist ending reveals murderer Angela is really a boy whose been forced to dress as a girl. (The final shot is of Peter/Angela covered in blood and showing, as one YouTube commenter puts it, "his tiny pee-pee.") The most well-developed girl in Grade Six (aka "Watermelons") wears an anklet on her right foot, which means she's done "it." The kid from down the street has *Playboy* pinups on his bedroom walls — his parents don't mind at all! He brings treasures to school: his mum's contraceptive pills, his dad's rubbers. None of these items appear in Sweet Dreams books, and Sweet Valley High only hints at them.

But I am prepared now. It's 1984. I'm going to the local Catholic high school. So far this year, I have entered a Madonna look-alike competition (not even a runner-up, and I wore Mum's black bra and everything!) and created a dance to the Mel Brooks song "To Be or Not to Be," incorporating forward tumbles. I have bundled up my Sweet Dreams and Sweet Valley Highs and sold them as a bulk lot in the Trading Post. (Amanda from Wantirna's dad said she would be rapt.) Romance still eludes me and will do so until I leave school. I have, perhaps, read too much of the wrong thing. But never mind—Jackie Collins is just around the corner, and Shirley Conran's *Lace* and Sidney Sheldon's *Master of the Game*. I will become a writer and my road will be paved with paperbacks that fall open on a certain page.

*Names have been changed.

Every Disgusting Detail
Benjamin Law

When you grow up with older siblings, you tend to read a lot of stuff that isn't exactly age appropriate. My sister Candy is six years older than me, so I would've been around ten when she started reading scandalous things like V. C. Andrews's *Flowers in the Attic* and novels by Christopher Pike. Younger brothers always want to copy their older siblings, but even I knew these mild horror stories of incest and murder were going to give me nightmares — or at least force me to imagine myself locked in an attic, slowly being poisoned with cyanide and making out with my sister. So I made an active effort to avoid those books.

Still, I dove into other sections of Candy's bookshelf, devouring her copies of *TV Hits, Smash Hits, Girlfriend,* and *Dolly* magazines. My favorite magazine section was of course Dolly Doctor, which published the anonymous medical queries of pubescent girls from across Australia, driven by anxiety, embarrassment, and a fear of imminent death. When the questions weren't about their copious quantities of vaginal discharge, they tended to focus on their fear of getting pregnant. I'd read them all, appalled and fascinated:

Dear Dolly Doctor,

I swam in the same pool as my brother last night, but he's older than me and is probably making sperm and now I'm worried his sperm might have gone inside me through the water. Can you get pregnant like this? HELP, I DON'T WANT TO HAVE MY BROTHER'S BABY.

Dear Dolly Doctor,

Before I get my period, a thick, gooey discharge oozes out of my vagina that's yellow and sort of snot-like in texture. AM I GOING TO DIE???

Dear Dolly Doctor,

Lately I've been getting really thick, slime-like discharge from my vagina, and I was wondering if—

Oh, my God, I'd think. *Does every girl get this much vaginal discharge?* But really, I loved every disgusting detail and kept on reading. Looking back, it probably wasn't the healthiest thing for a ten-year-old to consume.

It wasn't only *Dolly* that I poached from Candy's bookshelf. Tucked in between her horrible incest books and teen magazines, she also kept quite a few novels from her childhood. A lot of them were Enid Blyton books, but I had tried reading those already and found them insufferably boring, except for the fact that characters had names like Dick and Fanny. (*HAHAHAHAHA, IMAGINE BEING CALLED FANNY!*)

Another book looked promising, though. It was a slim kids' novel called *The Twits* by Roald Dahl. Published two years before I was born, the book was apparently inspired by Roald Dahl's acute hatred of men's beards, which he found unsightly. (Roald Dahl would have hated modern-day Melbourne.) I loved *The Twits* from the very first page. It was deliciously horrible: the tale of a husband and wife who lived together but loathed each other, and placed personal hygiene low on their priorities. Mr. Twit's beard was so bristly and big that all manner of stinky food got caught up in it: sardines, cheese, and cornflakes. Mrs. Twit only had one eye, and when she wanted to spook her husband, she'd put her glass eye in his drinking glass. I loved it all: the horrible, almost odorous descriptions of Mr. and Mrs. Twit; the scheming, vengeful cast of animals; and the practical jokes Mr. and Mrs. Twit played on each other, all of which would probably qualify as domestic violence nowadays.

I finished the book in a single sitting, then went right back to the start and read it all over again. Reading it as an adult now, I've also discovered some genuine wisdom sprinkled throughout, like how if a person had ugly thoughts, it'd begin to show on their face; Dahl added that if a person had good thoughts, they could never technically be truly ugly. You could have a wonky nose and a crooked mouth and a double chin and messed-up teeth, but if you had good thoughts, it would apparently shine out of your face like sunbeams and you'd always look lovely. This would prove to be comforting advice when I saw less-than-attractive people on the street. Plus I'd later develop acne so severe, I'd eventually need to go on a course of Roaccutane, so Dahl provided a good pep talk too.

Noticing my newfound love affair with *The Twits*, my mother went insane that Christmas and bought me a bundle of Roald Dahl books: *The Witches, James and the Giant Peach, George's Marvelous Medicine, Matilda, The BFG, Charlie and the Chocolate Factory, Fantastic Mr. Fox,* and *The Magic Finger.* Books were never seen as an extravagance in my family, and my mum lovingly inscribed every single inside cover (for instance, in *George's Marvelous Medicine:* "Do not do this to your mother!"). It's still the best present she's ever given me. I stayed indoors for months, reading those books.

Like all excellent kids' books, Dahl's had a thing for underdogs. There were orphans (James, who finds a giant peach; the unnamed protagonist in *The Witches; The BFG*'s Sophie), neglected children (Matilda), and really poor ones (Charlie Bucket). The villains were always vivid: a cast of horrible adults, from abusive headmistresses to satanic witches, horrible aunties, and criminal parents.

Nowadays, I'm a writer myself, but I don't write fiction or kids' books. I write about real people. But like Dahl, I'm attracted to outsiders and the strangeness of ordinary life, and Dahl's books taught me some key lessons in writing: to always look for the humor in tragedy, and to see the potential for adventure to spring out of misery. Earlier this year, I discovered that my favorite bookshop in Brisbane was selling official Roald Dahl mugs. For my boyfriend, I bought the *BFG* mug in honor of his favorite Dahl book. ("I always loved the idea that something could visit you in the night, and that it could be friendly, not scary or threatening," he says.) Personally, though, I couldn't choose a favorite. In the end, I picked the mug featuring Quentin Blake's illustration of George, from *George's Marvelous Medicine.* That mug—which I use nearly every day at my writing desk—reminds me that when it comes to writing, I should approach it as George would: chuck everything in and stir it around, understanding that it's all trial and error. And eventually, with the right chemical reaction, something magical might just happen.

Challenging the Machinations of Racism
Jared Thomas

My grandfather Jimmy Fitzpatrick (Pop Fitz)—my mum's dad—was the person who handed me the book that awakened my interest in reading.

There're a few images that come to mind when I think of my grandfather. One is of him smelling of beer and cigarettes, wearing his Australian National Railways denim, his steadfast hat, and carrying his tucker box and a couple of longnecks of beer as he got home from work.

Another is of Pop sitting at the Wilsden Football Club bar, drinking, smiling, or arguing as he talked politics. And the most enduring is of Pop, whenever he wasn't doing the other two things, reading.

When I was a teenager, I asked my pop if I could interview him for a school project where I had to write a biography. It was probably Mum's idea.

I learned how Pop was born in Winton, Queensland, in 1925 to Henry Fitzpatrick, an Irishman, and Hilda Dodd, an Aboriginal woman. Pop has an older sister, Adelaide, and three younger brothers. Until Pop was a teenager, he had grown up relatively wealthy. He was delivered by a doctor, which was unusual in those times, and went to the fancier Catholic school, and his cousins, the famous Cannings, were pastoralists. He had access to toys and paddocks to play in, but most important, this short-lived lifestyle gave him access to books.

My aunty Adelaide told me that when their grandparents came over from Ireland when Pop was about twelve, their father kicked their mum and all of the children out of the family home because my Irish great-great-grandparents were ashamed that their son had married an Aboriginal woman.

This experience along with other similar experiences led Pop to the conclusion that the world could be cruel and unfair, and that it was particularly the ideas that people possess about class, race, and sexuality that make it so. Pop was particularly focused on fighting class prejudice and discrimination in his lifetime. I think he drank those beers when he felt a bit overwhelmed by it all.

I hadn't really talked with or known Pop until that project, and I could tell that the connection that was established through it was bittersweet because it was only a matter of time before he would die. Not that my pop was sick or anything at the time—he'd just led a really hard life, and drinking and smoking were bound to cause damage.

My dad's father, Pop Rations (Raymond Thomas), a

Nukunu-Ngadjuri man, had died around this time, so Pop Fitz's death was also in the forefront of my mind.

Pop could see that I was particularly interested in talking about racism. I think I already had a pretty good understanding of it. Even as a kid I'd picked up that many non-Indigenous people in my hometown of Port Augusta thought of Aboriginal people as second-rate. When I was about fifteen the local council attempted to impose a curfew on local youth that seemed targeted at Aboriginal kids and would ultimately further deteriorate relations between the Aboriginal and non-Indigenous community.

My awareness of what my father's family had gone through due to being Aboriginal was growing. The other thing that was fueling my interest in the machinations of racism was the current-affairs show *60 Minutes,* which regularly reported on Nelson Mandela and apartheid in South Africa.

So maybe to stop my barrage of questions or having to talk about things that were painful, Pop gave me a copy of the novel *The Power of One* by Bryce Courtenay.

It looked so big. I thought it would take years to read. But I can still remember reading that book, during the early 1990s, lying in my bed in Port Augusta, hearing the freight train cross the salt lake.

The main character of *The Power of One* is a young white boy contending with the realities of South Africa as he grows into adulthood. The book is based on Courtenay's own experiences. He was banned from reentering South Africa after setting up a weekend school for black South Africans through his high school.

As I was drawn into the characters and their experiences, I developed a deeper understanding of the futility of racism and an appreciation for those who actively attempt to address it. I also felt surprise and a sense of satisfaction with how quickly I made my way through the book. Before reading the novel, I had only reluctantly read shorter works for school assignments.

Within a year or two of reading *The Power of One*, I watched the play *Funerals and Circuses* by Roger Bennett when I was on a school excursion in Adelaide.

My classmates and I stood out at the front of the theater without a clue about what we were going to see. There were two Aboriginal men trying to gain entry into the theater. The security team started giving the men a hard time. The men, who were well dressed and made a point of this, presented their tickets, but still the security tried to move them on. It was very clear to me why, but I felt incapable of doing anything about it. I'd also had a lifetime of seeing Aboriginal people being treated like rubbish without any recourse.

Very early into the performance of the play, the Aboriginal men who were moved on by the security team appeared on stage. They asked why the audience members hadn't jumped to their assistance. I found the experience mesmerizing. The singer-songwriter Paul Kelly performed in the play, and I was particularly impressed with the way non-Aboriginal people were working with Aboriginal people to show how racism was affecting Aboriginal Australia.

It was then and there that I decided to become a playwright and decided to knuckle down so that I could go to university and get some advice on how to go about it.

In one of my early uni tutorials we were supposed to discuss *No Sugar* by Western Australian Aboriginal playwright Jack Davis. Just when I knew there was a text on the curriculum that I felt comfortable discussing, the tutor refused to discuss the work, saying it was ridiculous that an Aboriginal text be read in a university English program. I protested, saying that the story contained within Davis's work was similar to that of my grandparents and I wanted to discuss it. I was questioned about this and criticized for not being black enough. I almost packed my bags and jumped on the first bus back to Port Augusta.

A few weeks later, I was reading *Summer Lightning and Other Stories* by Caribbean writer Olive Senior, and I knew that the non-Aboriginal students and staff delivering that English course were receiving Senior's work much differently than Davis's. This interested me because it really felt to me that Olive was speaking about my family and community; only the places she talked about and the accent of the people were different.

My first play, *Flash Red Ford,* a story based on the experiences of my Nukunu great-grandfather, was performed in Kenya and Uganda in 1999, shortly after Pop Fitz died. Roger Bennett read drafts of this play shortly before his death. Roger was a great influence for me. He had come from a very disadvantaged background, and knowing what he had produced without a classic high-achieving mainstream background gave me hope regarding how my writing might develop. I felt privileged and was grateful that Roger was so giving of his time and knowledge.

I later connected with people who had worked on Bennett's play. In 2001, I worked as second assistant director on the film *One Night the Moon* featuring Paul Kelly, and my 2002 play *Love, Land and Money* featured actors Robert Crompton and Michael Harris, the two actors who were refused entry into *Funerals and Circuses.* Beyond Bennett's play inspiring me to write, I continue to encounter people who have some connection to Roger, his play, and the people who worked on it. I come to collaborate with these people and they inspire and contribute to my development.

In this way, I've felt like *Funerals and Circuses* has played a magical role in my life.

I constantly revisited Olive Senior's *Summer Lightning and Other Stories*, and it inspired me to write fiction, at first short stories and then a novel. My first reading of the collection as well as observing how non-Indigenous readers responded to it kept me in university study. Further readings enabled me to understand the great craft involved in Senior's writing: how she produces pace and suspense, reveals contradiction, and stays true to the motivations of characters.

When I began writing the novel *Calypso Summer* in 2007, I decided to write to Senior to request her mentorship, particularly due to the references to the West Indies and Rastafarianism in the novel. I couldn't believe it when Olive agreed.

In 2008, I traveled with Olive through Jamaica and experienced the places she talks about in her work. Spending time with Olive helped me to understand the role and work of the writer and the type of discipline involved. The experience also highlighted the impact of colonization on black and Indigenous peoples and how literature plays an important role in assisting us to address issues. In 2009, Olive traveled to Australia and spent time with my family and me in Port Augusta. She was a neighbor to Bob Marley on Hope Road, Kingston, and knew him well. We are good friends. Olive is now in her seventies, and I am inspired to hear of her constant writing pursuits and travels around the world, presenting her work and teaching.

The texts that I mention above, *The Power of One* by Bryce Courtenay, *Funerals and Circuses* by Roger Bennett, and *Summer Lightning and Other Stories* by Olive Senior, undeniably changed my life.

When Pop Fitz handed me *The Power of One*, it wasn't like he was just handing me a book: he was handing me a way of looking at the world that he knew would serve me well given my experiences and interest. The awakening of my interest in reading has led to a profession that has assisted me to travel the world and form enlightening and enduring friendships.

The exciting thing is knowing there are writers and books out there that will push me in equally surprising directions in years to come.

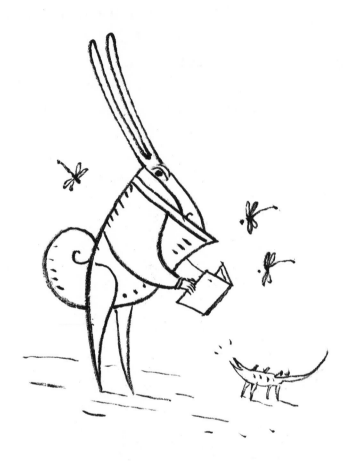

I enjoy seeing things from
a different point of view.

Invested with Enchantment
Alison Croggon

Every book that's ever mattered to me has changed my life. There are so many that it's hard to choose one. There are the books that formed thoughts I didn't know I had and opened doors to new ways of thinking, books that have haunted me for years and changed the color of my mind forever. Even books I hated have a place in showing me what I didn't want to do and didn't want to be. I am a writer because of every book I've ever read. And if you are a writer, you never stop finding new books to fall in love with. You never stop learning from other writers.

But out of all of them, perhaps the honor ought to go to J. R. R. Tolkien's *The Lord of the Rings*. I read it when I was ten years old in a single twenty-four-hour sitting. My parents had been fighting late at night, one of the interminable, bitter quarrels that marked the final years of their marriage, and I lay in bed listening. When they finally went to bed, I couldn't sleep. I got up and found *The Lord of the Rings* on the kitchen table and, for want of anything else to do, began to read it. I read it all night and all the next day, unable to put it down, enthralled by this complex, dangerous, and beautiful world that suddenly opened before me. Here were perils and marvels, grief and loss and conflict, but also the beauty of the natural world, the taste of bread, the importance of friendship. It was the world I knew, transfigured and invested with enchantment.

Perhaps it's not surprising, given how grindingly miserable I was for so much of my adolescence, that the world of *The Lord of the Rings* became an obsession for the next four or five years. I read everything by Tolkien I could get my hands on, including his more obscure stories—*Farmer Giles of Ham* and *Tree and Leaf.* The single-volume edition that I had first read became so tattered it was almost unreadable, and when my parents gave me a hardback three-volume edition I solemnly buried the old paperback in the garden. (I think I unburied it later.) For those years, I suspect that Middle Earth, with its high, graven language and its epic beauty, was the closest I ever came to religion.

I was a confirmed atheist by the age of seven: I simply couldn't bring myself to believe in the reality of God. Religion seemed to me so obviously a human invention. Perhaps as a result of this, I've always been fascinated by religious texts, from the Bible to the Upanishads, from the Judaic Kabbalah to the anonymous woman mystics of the Middle Ages. Some of my favorite poets are deeply religious. Perhaps I can understand the struggle for spiritual meaning, and for moral structure, but I can't understand why you have to invent a god. There have been times when I desperately wished I could believe in religion, but it offended my rationality. For me, unable to believe in any god, fantasy seemed more honest.

The Lord of the Rings was an escape, but if it had only been escapism, I don't think I would have been nearly as obsessed. It showed me that you could invent another world that could live and breathe in your imagination, and communicate that to others. What made *that* world most real were all the things that were real in my day-to-day realities. In *this* world, I could face my confusions and fears and unhappiness, transformed through the act of imagination into something that fed my hunger for beauty and meaning. And hope too.

The Lord of the Rings is certainly the book that made me a fantasy writer. I was fascinated by Tolkien's languages and scripts, and began to make up my own. I had written poetry from when I first began to form letters, but the desire to write an epic fantasy was my first real writerly ambition. From the beginning, I wanted to make up my own world, not to live in the one that Tolkien invented. Years later, when I heard of people who learned how to speak Quenya, one of the Elvish languages that Tolkien invented, I was baffled. The point, surely, was to make up your *own* language.

When I finished that first, enthralled reading, I immediately began to write a novel that was almost exactly the same as *The Lord of the Rings* (if it was written by a love-struck ten-year-old). I had a fountain pen with black ink, I remember, and a notepad with no lines on it in which I jealously wrote My Novel. I drew maps. I invented histories. It got to about a hundred pages long. At the stern, unsentimental age of fourteen, disgusted by my juvenile scribblings, I decided to divest myself of childish things and threw that notepad away. I've been sorry ever since. I'm sure it was terrible, but I'd love to still have it.

I grew up. Along the way, I read other books, many of which have been as formative as *The Lord of the Rings*. I began to wonder why all the heroes in the stories I read were male. I began to wonder why all the heroes were white. I published several books of poetry and wrote some operas and worked as a journalist. I had children, who grew up and began to read, and because they read the books I loved as a child, I reread them, and remembered how much they meant to me.

One day, thirty years after I'd first read those lines "Concerning Hobbits," I thought, why don't I write a fantasy novel? And that old ambition, the first I ever had, reignited. Over the next ten years I wrote the Pellinor quartet. To my surprise, having never written anything longer than a twenty-page opera libretto, I discovered I loved making up long stories. In the end, the four volumes of the Pellinor books added up to 2,000 pages. I have just finished another Pellinor book, which brings the total story to 2,500 pages. It only took me thirty years to begin, and another twenty to write. Writing books can take much longer than you think.

I know the writers I learned from in writing those stories. Tolkien is an obvious influence, although I rigorously excluded elves, dwarves, orcs, rings, and dragons. Another was Ursula Le Guin, whose Earthsea trilogy I read as obsessively as *The Lord of the Rings* through my teenage years.

The central idea for the Pellinor quartet came from Robert Graves's eccentric and fascinating book *The White Goddess,* which is actually about poetry. In *The White Goddess,* Graves decodes a fourteenth-century poem by the Welsh poet Taliesin, which he claims is a sacred alphabet and calendar, with each letter representing a tree and a season. That became the basis for the Treesong, the central metaphor in the Pellinor epic. A lot of poets I love are twined invisibly through the story, often as private jokes: the name of one of the major characters, Nelac, is an anagram of Celan, a twentieth-century German poet I admire. I know there are passages in which I wanted to create the same feeling I had in reading books by Alan Garner. I structured the books like dramas because that's what Dostoyevsky did with his novels.

And my hero was a girl, because when I was young, I never read books in which the epic heroes were girls. I always had to imagine that I was a boy.

Of course, the book you write isn't simply the sum of every book you've read. What makes it come to life is your experiences, real and imagined: all your sadnesses, all your joys, which you transform into the body of the story. Many other things changed my life: falling in love, falling out of love, having children, working, witnessing injustice and the struggles against it. I bring all those things to every book I write, because I can't help it. So many things have made me what I am, and all the time I am beginning again.

It Looks Like a Comic
Mal Peet

Well, it wasn't a particular book. It wasn't even books in general, much as I loved them. As soon as I could read, in fact, I went through my primary school's little library like a bookworm dipped in Red Bull. In part, this was because books were, to me, exotic. I did not come from a bookish family. There were few, if any, books in our house. Certainly no fiction, unless you count the Bible. This was not unusual. I grew up in a working-class council estate (subsidized housing) in the 1950s where spending money on books would have been seen as eccentric, if not actually irresponsible. Hence my greed for the stories in the library.

My parents were puzzled, even startled, by my bookishness, but, to be fair to them, they did not actively discourage it. When I was maybe eight or nine, my mum put away a few pence a week and subscribed to a mail-order book club called something like the Classics Library. Once a month or so, the postman would deliver a suspicious package and I, home from school, would rip it open to discover what new wonder it contained. I was frequently disappointed. I just couldn't get on with *Little Women*. And has anyone out there read, or tried to read, *The Children of the New Forest* by Captain Frederick Marryat? Well, bless you if you have.

Books with the word *island* in the title were generally more reliable.

Despite the clunkers, the actual *possession* of these books was thrilling. I spent hours arranging them on my bedroom windowsill. They were cheap editions (obviously, but hardback with colored jackets), and when you first opened them, they gave off a distinctive smell, something like the whiff of a recently deceased fish combined with boiled turnip. The aroma of literature.

If loving and owning books was a secret perversion in my peer group, the love and ownership of comics was universally shared. Ah, *comics*. Now we come to it.

When I was a kid, there were lots of comics and most families could afford one a week. They got delivered with the newspaper, Tuesdays and Thursdays. There were boys' comics and girls' comics. Boys' comics had manly names: *The Victor, The Rover, The Hotspur, Tiger*. The strips featured war heroes, sportsmen, detectives, pirates, spacemen, explorers: the adult heroes we would inevitably become. Girls' comics (which I furtively read) were mostly about gypsy ballet dancers, gymkhanas, and awkward girls in private schools. I found them intriguing and utterly baffling.

As soon as I was old enough (eleven, I think), I got a before-school job delivering newspapers on my bike. My motive was not financial. I just wanted to read all the comics before I poked them through letter boxes along with the papers. It's a wonder I wasn't killed, pedaling along with my eyes fixed on *Roy of the Rovers*, soccer star of Melchester Rovers. (It was a kick in the guts when I learned there was no such team as Melchester Rovers.)

So when I started writing my childhood stories, I naturally wrote them in the form of comic strips. I drew what happened, then put the story beneath the pictures and the dialogue in speech bubbles. I was, of course, completely unaware that I was absorbing ideas about form and narrative that would be invaluable to me as an adult writer. These are (forgive me if they are obvious): imagine the scene, visually, in detail, before you put a single word on paper or the screen; how to order dialogue and keep it short enough to fit into a bubble; the difficulty of interrupting the line of a story to do "flashbacks" ("dream bubbles" always annoyed me); that something has to happen or change in every scene. I also became aware that the little white spaces between each frame of a strip had a purpose. They told the reader that between the last picture and this one stuff had happened that the reader need not be told about or could imagine for themselves, like "cuts" in movies or TV. (My family didn't have television until I was well into my teens.) Today, white space (things left unsaid or mysterious) is something I think hard about and disperse tactically through my writing.

Comics, in short—and for better or worse—made me the writer I am.

Contemporary writers who did grow up familiar with the conventions of film and TV learned these lessons far more quickly, of course. Their problem is how to make books different from, rather than similar to, video.

In my early teens I discovered Classics Illustrated. These were comic-book versions of Great Works of Literature. I remember *The Three Musketeers*, *The Iliad*, *Great Expectations*. Most of all

I remember the Classics Illustrated version of *Moby-Dick* by Herman Melville. I guess if I was stood against a wall and asked at gunpoint to name the greatest novel in English I would have to say *"Moby-Dick."* But I first encountered it as a comic. The unsophisticated drawings of the white whale bursting out of the frames scared the shit out of me.

When I went to university to study American literature, I took the comic with me. And when we did a seminar on *Moby-Dick*, I took it with me and instead of the proper book I put the comic on the table. (I was an irritating little sod.) The professor was a serious and severe American. After a while he noticed my comic.

"What is that thing you have in front of you, Mr. Peet?"

"The Classics Illustrated version of *Moby-Dick*, sir."

"It looks like a comic."

"Yes, sir."

"Pass it down the table, please."

He studied it carefully and silently for several minutes. The other students slid their eyes back and forth.

The professor said, "Where did you obtain this, ah, version, Mr. Peet?"

I said, "From a newsagent's shop in Norfolk."

"I see," the prof said. "Tell you what, I'll give you five pounds for it."

Five pounds was a lot of money back then. More than a week's rent. I thought hard about it.

I said, "Thank you, but I'd rather keep it."

I've still got it, I hope, somewhere in the accumulated trash of my life.

I'm recharging my imagination.

My First Reader
Ursula Dubosarsky

Some children never stop reading.
I remember when I learned to read. I was six.
Slowly, strangely, the letters gathered meaning—
That procession of long-spotted necks—
"Giraffes" reaching upward across the page
Of my very first reader. *A Day at the Zoo*
With Jill and Ken. "Here is the cage
Of laughing monkeys—look!" says Father. Blue
Is Mother's dress, blue the sea, the sky.
Home in the yellow car, sunlight fading.
Shhh, Baby is asleep. Good-bye, good-bye!
The elephant's trunk is waving . . .

Words and pictures—the dream revealing—
That's why some children never stop reading.

In Folded Arms
Cath Crowley

I read *Zigzag Street* by Nick Earls one warm day while I was sitting on the verandah of a house I shared with three other people. It was early spring — pink air, a sharp blue sky — the kind of weather that a friend once said made him feel hopeful and sexy — two things that seemed far away as I sat in a deep wicker chair, unshowered and wearing pajamas.

I'm pretty sure I stole my copy. I can't remember from where — maybe a housemate that I lived with when I first moved to Melbourne. It definitely belonged to someone before me, and probably to a few people before them.

Over the years I've found all kinds of things in books — letters, shopping lists, bus tickets, dreams. I've found tiny spiders, flattened cigarettes, and stale tobacco in the creases. I found a condom once (wrapped and unused but ten years out of date — a story in itself). Mostly, people leave circles and lines, parts of themselves.

My copy of *Zigzag Street* has what looks like teeth marks near the spine on the front cover. There are two coffee rings on the title page, and an inscription from a past reader in purple pen and small letters: *Dear Chop, Hope this book brings you some relief, as it did me. Love Chop xxx*

I'd never met either of the Chops, and I never did. But I imagined they'd needed the same kind of relief as I did. I'd just broken up with someone. I don't remember the details, except to say that I was left feeling pretty shit, and if I'm honest, sort of insane.

I'd seen other friends go through that kind of insanity, the kind where you have to keep busy or you'll do something stupid like calling. And calling. And calling. And calling. And calling. The two of you saying terrible things to each other every time, wanting to get closer but getting further and further away.

I was in my early twenties, I think. Technically it was the second time I'd been dumped, but both times were by the same person, so in my memory I've squashed the two hurts together into the one event. It was definitely the first time I'd been in love and trying to get out of it.

I don't remember starting the book, the moment of picking it up and reading. I remember the author's inscription, though: *This is for SG, for support and foolishness, both without limit.* I'm fairly sure that I underlined the second part of it—but I can't remember doing it, so maybe it was someone who'd been unlimitedly foolish before me.

The book tells the story of Richard Derrington—he's doing it tough, the blurb tells us. Ann's trashed him and his job seems pointless. Tuesday, Richard tells us, seems moderately fucked by ten.

One of the Chops had marked that line. I marked it too. It was Sunday when I was reading, about midday, and my life seemed to be monumentally fucked. So that made four of us who'd been where I was—me, Chop, Richard (and, so I assumed, at least in part, Nick Earls).

I won't tell you the rest of Richard's story—except to say that the plot was nothing like my break, but the specifics, the feelings, the lines about music and takeaway food and loss and lunacy that can attack you, felt written for me. Of course they felt like that. Nick Earls is brilliant at capturing what it's like to be human.

Zigzag Street made me laugh. It kept me occupied, and in another world that was just to the left of mine for a day. The last line—read the book, read it—gave me that feeling I've had so many times since—momentum. Because the right words, in the right order and rhythm, mess with you in exactly the right way. Sentences written well point at things with their shape—here, look at this sadness. Here, look at this light.

There was the exact right combination of humor and insight in *Zigzag Street* that day. I felt stupid along with every other human in the world.

I'm pretty sure I chased it down with Nick Hornby's *High Fidelity* and Markus Zusak's Wolfe Brothers trilogy. Second-hand copies both of them, and marked up by ludicrous humans in love before me.

I haven't read *Zigzag Street* all the way through since then. I dip into parts of it, and I read the last line. It's sitting on my desk as I write this—the same copy that I held on the verandah that day. On the pages, invisible to other readers for the most part, but completely visible to me, is that day in spring; the house where I read it; Chop, who'd needed and read it before me; the person that I loved and was trying to forget; the person I would love after them—who arrived at the end of that spring.

I can still remember how I felt when I finished *Zigzag Street*. I was smiling, holding it in folded arms. I still felt a bit shit, sure. But at least I didn't feel so alone.

I like short stories.

What Would Edith Do?
Emily Maguire

I don't remember what made me buy *Grand Days* by Frank Moorhouse. Given that I was, as a teenager, constantly broke and constantly hungry for books, it's likely I picked it up because it was as thick as the mattress I slept on each night. Thick books meant days, rather than mere hours, of distraction and escape.

I'll be honest: if I'd known how much of this book was taken up with discussing the inner workings of the League of Nations, an ill-fated organization founded in 1920 to resolve international disputes without war, I probably wouldn't have given it a chance. Rereading it over the years, I've come to appreciate the humor with which Moorhouse describes the machinations of international diplomacy and am now moved by the soaring, though ultimately futile, sense of hope driving the League. When I was seventeen, however, world politics felt as relevant to my life as yak farming, so I mostly skimmed those bits.

What *did* feel urgently, thrillingly relevant were the adventures of the protagonist: Edith Campbell Berry, a young Australian woman who goes to Geneva in the 1920s to take up a post at the League. In the very first chapter she shares a meal on a train with the older, charming Major Ambrose Westwood and ends up pashing him in her private compartment. By chapter 3 she's firing an ivory-and-silver pistol, riding through the streets of Geneva dressed as a sexy cowgirl, and shagging Ambrose while he wears her silk underwear. I loved her instantly and would have trawled through any number of pages about committee meetings to get to her next daring escapade.

Being a voracious reader, I had, of course, come across many fictional heroines who did cool, adventurous stuff; what was different about Edith was that she was nothing special. She was clever, yes, and had the advantage of a good education, but she was not breathtakingly beautiful, impossibly talented, or born to royalty or great wealth. Despite being a decade older than me and living before my grandparents were born, I related to her instantly and entirely. She was the role model I didn't even know I'd been searching for. She was who I wanted to be when I grew up.

I can't emphasize enough how significant this was. Although I was lucky enough to have some truly wonderful women in my life, I didn't have any role models for ambition and adventure. Within me there had always been this drive to seek out new lands, to explore new ideas, to collect experience just for the sake of it, but no one I knew did any of those things. Because of that, I'd gotten the idea that people who did amazing things were themselves naturally amazing. They were brilliant, brave, wellborn, breathtakingly beautiful, knowledgeable about everything, and never doubted themselves. In other words, I had the idea that adventure was not for the likes of me.

And now here was this fictional heroine: Edith Campbell Berry, who was, in terms of talent and beauty and courage, an awful lot like me, and who constantly chucked herself into situations she wasn't prepared for and might not be able to handle. What's more, her tendency to rush in and stuff things up was not treated in this glorious book as a failing or a sign that she was too big for her boots; it was shown as an intentional and marvelous way of living.

This was momentous. I had been raised to be ultra-aware of every risk. I wasn't allowed to walk home from school or ride a bike and was constantly warned about the dangers of choking, drowning, being kidnapped, hitting my head, breaking a bone, or catching a rare, permanently disfiguring disease. My mum would call out "Don't get hit by a car" literally every time I went anywhere there might be roads to cross. By the time I finished primary school, I was scared of pretty much everything and everyone.

At twelve I started at an exclusive, selective high school and began to absorb a different kind of fear: the fear that the rest of my life was being unalterably affected by every single thing I did. Every piece of homework, every exam, every question answered in class counted. Miss one day of school, mess up one test, or hand in one assignment late and I would have started the terrible downhill slope that ends in dropping out of school, working behind a fast-food counter, and living in a cockroach-infested slum.

By fourteen I was alternately paralyzed by terror about my future and driven manic by the feeling I was wasting my life. I ricocheted between playing perfect daughter and rebel-without-a-cause. I was a frightened, confused, angry mess of a girl, and by sixteen the terrible predictions came true: I was indeed a high-school dropout supporting herself behind a McDonald's counter (no cockroach-infested slum, but I was sure it was coming).

It was a terrible time. I'd quit school and cut my parents out of my life because I wanted to be free, only to find myself more restricted than ever. I had to work three jobs so I could make enough money to pay my rent and have some left over for books and alcohol. The books and alcohol were essential: my only means of escaping the grim, disappointing reality I'd created for myself.

And then, along came Edith and her realization that

She needed now in her life to put herself in a position which made her productively nervous. Even if it was a bit uncomfortable at times. She had to be where she didn't know quite what was happening next, to be living precipitously. She wanted to be in the presence of people who made her a little nervous. She wanted to be among objects, buildings and art works which made her mindful and sentient, which could cause her, now and then, to be in awe.

And something clicked. No, *clicked* is too mild a word. Something kicked. Smashed. Exploded. I hadn't ended up in a mess because I'd taken risks; I'd ended up a mess because the risks I'd taken were small, meaningless acts designed to show I was capable of rebellion while never forcing me to actually push beyond my own limits.

While I was still absorbing all this, another passage from *Grand Days* slapped me across the face:

It was a nonsensical paradox, to talk of planning for the unforeseeable. Life was a series of agile responses. How to modify the response precisely enough was the trick. Life was not technique. It was knack and artistry.

Oh! Planning for the unforeseeable was nonsensical? Of course it was! Which meant that the adults who told me I'd ruined my life by leaving school couldn't actually *know* that. The future—*my* future—was *unforeseeable!*

These ideas popped and crackled in my mind: risk and nervousness could be things to chase after; living a good life meant sometimes being in awe, and sometimes throwing myself into situations in which I couldn't foresee the outcome. These things had never, ever occurred to me. Once they did, I was on my way.

I won't claim that *Grand Days* alone changed my life or made me who I am—there were other books and writers and, most important, experiences that mattered as much or more. What *Grand Days* did was kick-start me by providing a role model, someone not terribly unlike me who decided to tackle life head-on.

For a time in my late teens and early twenties, I would, when facing a big decision or difficult situation, ask myself "What Would Edith Do?" I did it when deciding to go back and complete my education despite feeling terrified that everyone would look down on me for being a loser dropout who always smelled like French fries. I did it when deciding to camp my way around Europe in the middle of winter (the only time I could afford to go). I did it in campgrounds and bars and train stations and airports around the world. I did it when trying to find the courage to send my first novel—a document I had sweated blood over every night for a year and which nobody even knew existed—to a publisher.

I did it so often it became part of my thought process. I did it until I was living in such a way that I no longer needed Edith's example: I had become the heroine of my own life. Never mind what Edith *would do*, look what Emily *is doing*!

I didn't think about Edith for a long time. I kept doing stuff that would have blown the mind of teenage-me. I had this living-large thing totally under control. And then, not so long ago, I found myself in an austere, cavernous Communist Party meeting hall in the remote mountains of Northeast Vietnam, in a room full of dignitaries, including several high-ranking officers in the former North Vietnamese Army. Abruptly, I was pulled to my feet and pushed toward the microphone to make a speech. My first thought was "Goddamn it, Emily, this is what you get for jumping into a military van with a bunch of poets with whom you're unable to communicate beyond 'cheers.' Time to fake a fainting fit and get the hell out of here."

My second thought was calm and clear: "What Would Edith Do?" Well, she would speak, of course. So I did. As I could speak no Vietnamese and no one there could speak English, I'm still not sure why I was asked to address the group or why they applauded my unintelligible speech so enthusiastically. Perhaps they were simply admiring the "knack and artistry" with which I approached a daunting situation.

Later that day as I drank home-brewed rice whiskey in the back room of the local political head honcho's house—where I had been taken to view his teapot collection (yes, really)—I paused in my "series of agile responses" to reflect on what a marvelous life I was living. I made a toast to Edith, and the elderly Vietnamese men around me raised their glasses, and I knew that Edith would be terribly pleased.

I like BIG stories.

Putting the World to Rights
Catherine Mayo

I was only six or seven when I first discovered Barbara Leonie
Picard's *The Odyssey of Homer*. It was Christmas, the sun was
blasting down, and I was sitting on a New Zealand beach, itching
to go for a swim.

It all happened because my mother had a theory about cramps.
The theory went like this: if you swam with your tummy full
of food, you got cramps and drowned. Lunch was the obvious
danger meal.

To keep me and my two brothers safe from certain death,
Mum had to be pretty cunning. Every school holidays we'd spend
all day, rain or shine, at Sandy Bay on Waiheke Island, swimming
or mucking about in boats.

We kids weren't too fussed about cramps. Cramps were
something weird that happened to other people—old people.

It was years and years later that I found out that Granddad's best friend had drowned. He'd gone for a swim one afternoon and died. I don't know how long it was after lunch, but I'm not surprised Mum was a bit nervous on the subject.

Her trick was to read aloud. She was a good reader, and the books she chose — *Swallows and Amazons, The Hobbit,* the Narnia books, and Barbara Leonie Picard's retelling of *The Odyssey* — were always gripping and often attracted half the kids on the beach. After the post-lunch chapter from the current book-to-stop-us-coming-to-a-horrible-end, we were allowed back in the water.

The night reading session was also special. There was no bathroom in our tiny holiday cottage — not even any hot running water. At bedtime, Mum would boil a jug and we'd wash our faces, hands, and feet (in that order) in a tin basin. Then we'd tuck ourselves up in our sleeping bags in the kids' bedroom, waiting to be read to.

First off, we'd take turns bouncing the person in the top bunk. The mattresses were supported by woven wire mesh, so we could lie on the bottom bunk and shove the upper mattress up and down with our feet. That wire mesh got pretty saggy — it was a bit like sleeping in a hammock. Once Mum could take control of the situation, she'd read another chapter.

Sometimes Dad would take her place. Dad was hopeless. He was a scientist, specializing in plant diseases. He was also a terrible tease — a bad combination. If the hero or heroine was walking through a pine forest, Dad would have them stop in horror at the sight of a dying *Pinus radiata* tree, infected with *Phytophthora cinnamomi.* If they went into a garden, they'd find a glasshouse full of tomato plants riddled with blight.

"*Daaad,*" we'd yell in fury, "it doesn't say that."

"Oh, yes, it does," he'd answer, holding the book out of reach so we couldn't grab it and check.

"No, it does not," we'd shout. Mum, a stickler for the written text, would be summoned and Dad would get the sack.

Because I was the only girl and the youngest, Mum had to find books that would appeal to us all. One summer I insisted on *Heidi*, but my brothers vetoed it after two chapters. Or maybe it was only one. The Swallows and Amazons series, on the other hand, was a big favorite, perfect for a bunch of outdoor kids who loved boats. My eldest brother was so inspired by their adventures that he became a keen, competitive sailor.

Much as I loved the books, I never imagined myself as one of those kids. They were English, they went to some posh boarding school, and their sailing adventures mostly took place on an English lake that was very different from the ragged seacoast I knew so well.

It was Barbara Leonie Picard's retelling of *The Odyssey* that really captured my imagination. Odysseus's wanderings — all those encounters with one-eyed giants, six-headed monsters, ghosts, and sorceresses — took place on or near the sea. The small beaches, reef-bound harbors, rocky shores, and scrubby headlands around Sandy Bay were easy for me to transform into the scenes of Odysseus's various adventures.

One summer some friends announced they were going to sail their yacht down to Waiheke and visit us. So every day my brother Denis and I would climb up a narrow gorse-lined track to the top of the headland between Sandy Bay and Hekerua. There was an open grassy spot right on the snout of the headland, and we'd sit there watching out for our friends' keeler to come sailing in.

Or rather, Denis would be looking out for the yacht and I'd be Odysseus marooned on Ogygia and waiting to be rescued, or Penelope gazing out to sea, praying for Odysseus's ships to appear over the horizon.

When I was old enough to take a sailing dinghy out on my own, my daydreams became even more vivid. The little P class became Odysseus's raft, and I'd crouch in the cockpit, one hand on the tiller and one on the sheet, feeling the pull and heave of the wind and water as I stared across the bay at the local village of Oneroa and my imaginary homecoming.

I didn't restrict myself to the stories Homer told. There's a large element of fantasy, of fairy tale, about Odysseus's Wanderings that, right from age six or seven, led me into inventing my own variations on this old Greek story. One early invention of mine—which I don't feel any need to turn into a book now—had Odysseus go back to the Cyclops's cave after all his wanderings were over.

Why you'd want to make friends with a one-eyed monster who'd torn the heads off six of your mates and eaten their bodies in front of you is beyond me. I guess, as a young kid, I wanted to put the world to rights. Friendship is important, and healing little misunderstandings like this seemed a good idea at the time.

Back home in Auckland, I'd drive the family mad by shutting myself in the bathroom. Safely inside with the bolt across, I'd drape myself in a couple of towels knotted at the shoulder or fastened with safety pins to make an improvised tunic. There I would fight imaginary battles against Trojans and monsters while the family pounded on the bathroom door.

And at night I'd lie awake in bed in the dark and continue telling myself my stories about Odysseus. I even took to hiding bits of bread and cheese under my pillow—the closest I could get to an ancient Greek hero's diet—so Odysseus could enjoy a meager meal after days of starvation at sea.

What was it that hooked me on Odysseus?

Well, he was often outnumbered by enemies with brute force and magic on their side—an ancient Greek David to their Goliath. Maybe I saw him as a kindred spirit, as I battled to hold my own against two older brothers. Was that why I drove my eldest brother crazy (Laurie was definitely a monster in disguise) with my smart-arse remarks?

Or maybe it was just the power of Odysseus's personality—cunning and brave, resourceful and adaptable, quick on his feet, imaginative, a bit lippy, good at keeping secrets (too good sometimes), loving, and very loyal.

Did Odysseus instill in me my sense of adventure, my urge to give things a go, my competitiveness, determination, thoroughness, plain stubbornness, and initiative? Or did seeing those qualities in him feed what was already there in me?

What about those fabulous illustrations by Joan Kiddell-Monroe? I'm a sucker for pictures, and even by the time I was reading Dickens, I still adored the old-fashioned drawings, pausing to absorb as much of the detail as I could before reluctantly continuing with the text. In Picard's *Odyssey,* Kiddell-Monroe has a glorious picture of Odysseus greeting the ghosts in the Underworld. My hero's calf muscles are so impressively drawn that I spent the rest of my childhood, all my teens, and much of my twenties trying to grow muscles to match.

Or was it Picard's—and Homer's—talent for storytelling, the seduction of entering another world so vividly drawn, that inspired me?

Most young kids have strong imaginations and spend hours inventing stories and acting them out. But as we get older and busier, with homework and sport and remedial maths and music after school, with mates and projects and study and partners and jobs and rent and mortgages and our own kids later on, the everyday world crowds into our heads and stifles our imaginations.

The key, for a writer, is to keep that imaginative world alive, and in that way I was lucky. Somehow my Odysseus stories kept enticing me into their grip, and eventually I decided I had to write them down and share them.

I can take my time.

Beyond the Influence
Ted Dawe

The story was paid out like fishing line by my grandmother as she drove us about on prodigious car journeys. How young Dick Herron the Mountie and the wily old trapper Sam Bolton caught the renegade Ojibway Indian Jingoss and brought him back to face the consequences. It was a long story with many sidetracks about the frozen north of Canada, caribou herds, the Hudson's Bay Company, moccasins, and snow blindness. It pitted youth and vigor against age and experience. The trapper against the native. Loyalty to one's companions was balanced against loyalty to one's mission.

Growing up in the 1950s, car journeys around New Zealand were slow and taxing. It was particularly torturous for children, sitting in hot cars while we wound over endless dusty roads in elderly DeSotos or Ford Populars. My grandmother was an enthusiastic driver who had a tool bag full of tricks to pacify fidgety kids. She would let the favored front-seat passenger steer while we rolled down long hills with the engine switched off. She would sing "Lazybones" or "Down by the Canebreak." She would tell us funny stories about our mothers or fathers, the things they did when they were small. Most of all, though, she had the ability to retell a long novel in intricate detail.

The Silent Places, as I have discovered, was written by Stewart Edward White in 1904. The author was a prolific writer who specialized in stories set in the wilderness and in accounts of "channeling" or spiritualism. I only know this because modern technology (Wikipedia and Project Gutenberg) has put me in touch with the source material. Prior to this the book lived only in the form of car-borne narratives.

Sitting in my study today, with a fresh reprint of the novel in front of me, I see on the first page a couple of sentences that maybe sum up the book's early magic.

> *It was strange speech, richly embroidered with the musical names of places, with unfamiliar names of beasts, and with unintelligible names of things. Kenógami, Mamátawan, Wenebógan, Kapúskasíng, the silver-fox, the sea-otter, the sable, the wolverine, the musk-ox, parka, babiche, tump-line, giddés,—these and others sang like arrows cleaving the atmosphere of commoner words.*

Many years after these journeys, I discovered I had an affinity for books set in wildernesses of one sort or another, the novels of Jack London in particular. I imagine that these kinds of books had the same sort of appeal in the early 1900s (when my grandmother was a girl) as science fiction or fantasy does for today's young reader: the vicarious pleasure derived from journeys into uncharted lands and the challenges confronted there.

Looking at the book now, from a "fifty years later" vantage point, it seems incurably colonialist, racist, sexist, and any number of other "ists." The characters, and in particular the heroes, are caricatures of stalwart virtue, while the supporting cast are not so much people but part of the environment. The Indians ("Injuns"), the trappers, the wolverines, and the caribou: all obstacles to be overcome rather than carrying an individual truth or vitality. So given this, why does the story live on so sharply in my memory?

For the last ten years or so, I have been busily engaged in the art of novel writing. My books deal with teenage males in situations where they have passed well beyond the influence of their parents and have to cope in a challenging environment. Some of the decisions they make are life-or-death ones. Most are life changing. The language these characters speak will one day soon seem as antiquated as that spoken by Dick Herron and his trusty companion. The world they live in is largely urban, rigorously New Zealand in its character.

For all that, I struggle with the same artistic challenges that confronted White in the early 1900s. Authenticity, vitality, and relevance. My books are journeys of exploration into a world not often written about by other authors, and as a result, they attract controversy. I am pushing my way beyond the civilized world into a place that is largely uncharted, a place where I am constantly discovering things which frighten and amaze. Like young Dick Herron, my first duty is to my mission and my resolve is only strengthened by rebuke or criticism.

My grandmother grew up in a world only one generation removed from colonization. Her parents traded axe heads and blankets for farmland. England was her home, although she had never been there. Her education ceased at primary-school level. Despite that, she grew up to travel the world and become the revered matriarch to twenty-six grandchildren. She was fiercely opposed to swearing, sexuality, and bad manners. (My books are drenched with these things.) Yet this woman narrating this book is the single most important factor in my becoming a writer. Now, from the perspective of late adulthood, I have a few ideas about why this might be the case.

Oral stories rely on structure and memory devices in order to hold the reader. The structure of *The Silent Places* is fairly conventional: the hero, the quest, the outcome. This seems to fit with some instinctual template that our minds find satisfying. What makes the story memorable is the sharp specific detail (snow blindness, scalping, spoor); tension (the battle for survival of the warm-blooded in extreme cold); poignant themes (Dick Herron's love for a girl of an "inferior" race). My grandmother's voice glided over the ornate writing, accelerating or digressing as she sensed her audience's responses. All these things help the listener lose himself in the story and shuck off the tedium of daily existence.

In my writing I strive, like my grandmother, to hold my audience, to ring true, to captivate. Once that happens, then the narrative can roam far and near and the reader will float along in its wake. There is magic in this. I have never been able to resist its call. I believe I am not alone, that people like me are drawn to the altar of the keyboard, the tyranny of the blank page, to practice what the poet Dylan Thomas called our craft or sullen art.

rarf!

A Sense of Resolution
Simon French

A few short years ago, I found and purchased a secondhand copy of *The Silver Sword* by Ian Serraillier.

It was almost four decades since I had first discovered and read it, yet my recall of the characters and events remained as vivid as familial memory. Before affording *The Silver Sword* a deserving place on my bookshelves, I sat down to read it again, curious about my adult's reaction to the text and keen also to place Serraillier's work in the context of my life as an educator and author.

The Silver Sword, first published in 1956, tells of a Polish family, the Balickis, in the final stages of World War II. The opening chapter begins in the style of old-fashioned storytelling and character introductions, but with events, place, and characters introduced, the narrative quickly assumes greater speed and immediacy. The Balicki family is separated—father from family, and then the mother as well, leaving the three children to fend for themselves in the hostile environment of a turbulent wartime Europe.

My own copy of *The Silver Sword* is a hardback reprint from 1965, ironically the very edition I borrowed from Blacktown Library as an eleven-year-old in 1968. The edges of the pages are a little fragile; they are beginning to fox with yellow specks and are slightly grimed by dozens and dozens of page-turning fingers, including my own from long ago—and again more recently. When the municipal library moved to a brand-new building some years ago, much old and surplus stock was put out on sale tables in the foyer of the original building. And there I found several actual copies of books from my childhood, including Mr. Serraillier's landmark novel.

I think it may have been a review and extract in *The School Magazine* that first alerted me to *The Silver Sword*, but there was then another motivation behind wanting to find and read this story: my father had been in Bomber Command during World War II, and like many men of his generation, it was not something he talked about. Along with sex and any politics to the left of Sir Robert Menzies, "the War" was off-limits as a conversation topic in the household of my childhood.

Prior to *The Silver Sword*, the only fleeting encounter I'd had with the War was the arrival of the Nazis toward the end of the movie *The Sound of Music*. Age eight, I'd asked some innocent question about "those soldiers." My father furnished a brief reply, and something in the tone of his voice and answer piqued my curiosity. A couple of years later, when I brought *The Silver Sword* home from the library, the book earned itself a quiet nod of approval from him. I didn't realize at the time that I was embarking on a conscious voyage of discovery about my father as a young man, but I knew at the very least I was about to begin broadening my knowledge of the War.

And once I started reading, I could barely put the story down. I was *there*. Like so much great writing for children, the young protagonists have to strike out on their own, solve many of their own problems, be ever watchful for dangerous adults—and survive. Ruth, Edek, and Bronia face constant danger in their trek across war-torn Europe as they search for their father. The chance encounter with orphaned Jan reveals the fact that their father is alive and also searching for them. For Jan is in possession of a letter opener, a small silver sword given to him by an escaped prisoner of war—the Balicki children's father.

Serraillier's knowledge and detail of life, indeed childhood, during wartime remains an astonishing achievement. First published just eleven years after the conclusion of World War II, *The Silver Sword* must have been about the first piece of quality writing for children that depicted both the exciting and mundane experiences of boys and girls in the stressful, atypical circumstances of a comparatively recent conflict. Of course, many other fine works set in World War II have been published since—Robert Westall's *The Machine Gunners*, Penelope Lively's *Going Back,* Judith Kerr's *When Hitler Stole Pink Rabbit,* and Morris Gleitzman's series of novels beginning with *Once*—that are quite closely related to Serraillier's work, all with child protagonists negotiating a landscape that can be utterly dangerous at every step.

The Silver Sword, however, spares us the graphic aspects of war. In fact, it steers a path through a war zone largely uncluttered by blood and gore; awful certainties hover at the edges of each page, but we do not encounter them. We worry constantly about the safety of these children, feeling that their journey is ours as well. The reader desperately wills the Balickis to survive through sheer dint of their own humanity. Their determination, measured optimism, and kindness shine through all fraught interactions.

In the bedroom of my childhood, I hung on every paragraph of the Balicki family's journey, and felt great relief when sanctuary was found. Yet I felt a little disappointed as well: I really liked the character of Jan—the clever criminality that had helped him survive a war zone, his status as an orphan. There was a lot I liked about his enigma, and a lot more I wanted to know about him. I loved this mystery—that we never found out anything more about his background and the obvious trauma and loss that Serraillier hints at but skillfully sidesteps. The story's postscript is the very last page inhabited only by a portrait of Jan—well dressed, smiling, and serene. The portrait summed up the courage and inner reserves of strength that Jan and the Balicki children had mustered to reunite a family and to find peace for themselves. This happy conclusion to *The Silver Sword* is the best and only way that Ian Serraillier could have set out for his characters. For me, however, it is Jan's untold story as an orphan and child refugee that is the enticing and unfinished narrative.

Aspects of Jan have probably found their way into many of the narratives I've fashioned as an adult author. *The Silver Sword* was one of the childhood books that helped me include in my character casts not only kids who resembled my friends or students, but also the outsiders, delinquents, and enigmas. I taught myself to afford these latter personalities the same depth and empathy as I did my lead character or narrator—in fact, the outsiders often have been my narrators. I learned how to fashion a narrative that would leave the reader with a sense of resolution, with an understanding that the trajectory of a narrator's life would be strengthened and resolved by whatever experience had carried them through the course of a novel. As an adult writer, I came to understand how much my unfolding skills as an author had been indelibly fashioned by encountering so much in the way of quality reading, that reading and writing are so eloquently knotted together and dependent on one another.

For every one book I could have cited as the "book that made me," I could have listed a multitude of others: the works of E. L. Konigsburg, Patricia Wrightson, Penelope Lively, and Ivan Southall are but one quartet of favorites among many, many more that I read and loved as a child.

But it was the personal, family aspect that has shaped this appreciation of the one special book: my father. In his final years, he opened up a little more about his war experiences. He consented to answer the school assignment questions of a friend's teenage son, who in turn had the good sense to record his voiced answers. To me, my father in his last years made an uncharacteristic confession: that in England during the war he had enjoyed the company of a number of girlfriends, in particular a Danish girl whose family had fled to England. Several small black-and-white photos were produced, accompanied by an unfamiliar and warm commentary from my father. He then began to mention the bombing runs over Germany and in particular over Dresden. There was a certain intonation that crept into his voice at this point: grief and guilt, most likely for the devastation caused on the ground and for the many innocent lives lost. He did not live to read of the rebuilt Dresden Cathedral; I think such news would have meant a great deal to him.

What was left to me were over a hundred of the young Reg

French's war letters to his mother and sisters. And so I have his copperplate handwriting and the voice of a man barely out of his teenage years. I have his stories of life on the ground at an air base in Northern England, as well as his life in the air, as a wireless operator in a Lancaster bomber. Reg flew thirty-six missions over Europe, and because the attrition rate in Bomber Command was so high, he was lucky to have survived. On the ground, the Balicki children and thousands of others like them, suffered many privations but were also lucky to have survived among so many deaths. *The Silver Sword* provided a neat parallel to a slice of my family history. And when my father saw me reading this book—and the other World War II stories and historical accounts I went on to read throughout my high-school years—I think he saw that despite what I considered to be his shortcomings as a parent, I understood and appreciated the young years he had sacrificed to fight in a war in a place far from home, that I was interested in delving not only into history, but also into his head and heart. I wanted to know a little of who my father had once been, and how a war had changed who he later became.

The Silver Sword will always position itself thus in my reading life. Even the mere sighting of its spine among the many others on the bookshelf takes me to the landscapes—geographic and familial—that I've described. And *The Silver Sword* has in its own special way taken me everywhere in the years across my subsequent life as a writer.

It turns a boring commute into an ADVENTURE.

Only White People Lived in Books
Catherine Johnson

W e didn't have many books at home. *The Encyclopaedia Britannica* that my parents bought with the saved-up emergency-plane-fare-to-Jamaica fund, the Bible, some Welsh-language novels, and a few books of poetry by Caribbean writers.

But I had a library ticket and I was lucky with my timing: I was born in the early sixties, just when Dr. Seuss was making his way east across the Atlantic.

I owe him pretty much everything when it comes to words.

I think because my mother's first language was Welsh, she had very little knowledge of English children's books and neither did my Jamaican dad, who'd had a short, if classical, English education: Shakespeare and Wordsworth, but not E. Nesbit or Kenneth Grahame. So the books that were my own were, like me, from the second half of the twentieth century. I still have the well-beloved and dog-eared, battered hardbacks of *One Fish Two Fish Red Fish Blue Fish*, *The Cat in the Hat*, and *Green Eggs and Ham*.

Those books, read to me at bedtime, taught me to read. They must have done, because I can never remember not reading. I could read before I went to school; it was one of those things that came naturally, like breathing. I was very, very lucky. There are plenty of things I can't do — most of them involve throwing and catching and maths.

I have to admit I have an order of liking. *One Fish Two Fish Red Fish Blue Fish* comes first. The page at the back with Clark (who lived in the park) was so scary I had to sometimes skip it. But the Zans and Zeds, and Mike who was on hand to get the bike up hills (how I could use a Mike on my bike!) are still as heavily imprinted on me as the feeding of the five thousand. (I had a little hardback Bible story of that.)

After *One Fish* comes *Green Eggs and Ham*. I felt a well of empathy for poor Sam I Am, desperately trying to get his green eggs and ham eaten, and I loved the precipitous railways and the fox in a box and the mouse in a house.

The Cat in the Hat was most annoying. The Cat is spoiled, he doesn't listen, and he's such a terrible show-off.

But those wonderful rhyming picture books opened the door to a deep love, in my young self, of rhyming poetry. I can remember, age five or six, receiving for Christmas not the pony that I dreamed of but Louis Untermeyer's *The Golden Treasury of Poetry*. (Who is Louis Untermeyer? Should I google him? Will I be disappointed?) There were line drawings on every other page — the flag-draped skull from "The Battle Hymn of the Republic" was always scary. And I found the stylized fat-cheeked children illustrating "Isabel Jones and Curabel Lee" horrible in a different sort of way. I didn't like their eyes or cheeks and had to turn the page quickly there too.

My favorite poem was "The Ballad of Beth Gelert," about Prince Llewellyn's dog Gelert, who is killed by accident. It was very long and very tragic. I would recite this—reciting was big in Welsh households—although it must have been wearisome for my poor parents, as it was so very long. Perhaps I had more in common with the show-off Cat in the Hat than I would admit.

From classics to funny verse. Spike Milligan was famous off the telly, and his book *Silly Verse for Kids* was one I bought with my own money. I found it recently when we moved house and didn't like it half as much as I remembered it. Although I can still remember poems from that book too.

And after Spike Milligan came Edward Lear. Another Christmas, another poetry compendium, all of the limericks and poems. I can still do "The Owl and the Pussycat" off by heart, and parts of "The Nutcrackers and the Sugar-Tongs":

"Must we drag on this stupid existence for ever,
So idle and weary, so full of remorse,—
While every one else takes his pleasure, and never
Seems happy unless he is riding a horse?"

Novels, storybooks, came later, although there is one highly colored collection of fairy tales I liked, A4 size and hardback, with swan princes flying past a tower, and a history book with an illustration of Queen Mathilda on a very luxurious snowy-white horse.

The first novel I remember that was chosen and paid for with pocket money was *Comet in Moominland* by Tove Jansson. I bought it in Aberystwyth on a particularly boring holiday. Then there were the Edward Eager books *Half Magic* and *Magic by the*

Lake, set in pre–World War II America, about a single-parent family of four children who are poor—but not so poor that they don't have servants—and who happen upon a wish-giving magic coin. I remember distinctly liking the fact that one of the children was called Katharine, even though, to my mind, she spelled her name wrong.

Our schoolteacher in what would now be Years Five and Six—Mrs. Salter, thank you very much—read to us in the afternoon. We would sit on the hard parquet floor and she would read loads of stories. One I can remember hating at the time is *Emil and the Detectives,* although I have since read it and think it's fantastic. I don't know why that didn't click—was it a hot summer and hard to keep still? Maybe it was the lack of girls.

I also remember being steered toward Leon Garfield's books and not enjoying them either. I know it was pigheadedness on my part; I can remember standing in the book corner and looking at the crosshatching on the covers and putting the books back. Can I apologize for my stubborn ten-year-old self and say that as an adult I rate him as one of my favorite authors?

The only other novels I remember reading were a few Secret Sevens and Noel Streatfeild's *Gemma,* which I bought because the girl on the cover had great boots and the colors of that cover were really modern—acid green and brown and orange (it was the seventies). I did read *Ballet Shoes,* too, and how I wished wished, wished to be genteelly poor and super talented. But my default reading was the *Armada Book for Girls,* nonfiction, useful facts, and a lot of Things to Make and Do–style books. I also coveted my brother's books about Native Americans—full of how to make feather headdresses and full-size tepees, how to carve reproduction buffalo horns from wood, and step-by-step outlines of all the dances, although I don't think we ever made anything at all.

I liked stories from the cinema and from the TV. I loved *The Amazing Mr. Blunden* and the Sunday-afternoon serials like *The Little Princess* (I cried buckets). We would play those stories in school and there would always be an argument about who I would be. There was never anyone dark skinned enough. . . .

Is that why I sort of gave up on novels? I wonder. I never ever expected to see myself in a book. When I was growing up in the sixties and seventies, unbelievable as it seems now, I didn't know any other mixed-race kids—even in London we were rarer than hen's teeth. There was another black kid in my year, and there were Greek Cypriot kids and Jewish kids, but mixed race? Nope, nuh-uh, no way.

And anyway everyone back then knew only white people lived in books and had adventures. Even if there were black children, or dark-skinned ones, you wouldn't want to be them; they were at best the stupid sidekick or at worst the enemy. Magic only happened to white kids; only white kids rode ponies or sailed boats or went back in time or wore fantastic dresses. In late-sixties/early-seventies London, these were inalienable and unassailable truths. Who would want to play being black? After all, it was one more steep storybook rung below—horror of horrors—being a useless girl.

I didn't start reading children's books again until I was at college: all the Noel Streatfeilds, all the pony books, all the adventure and magic books. E. Nesbit, then Nina Bawden—I'd seen *Carrie's War* on telly—and Alan Garner—*The Owl Service*—I'd seen that on telly too. Jan Mark, and right up-to-date with Jacqueline Wilson and Aidan Chambers. I didn't start writing myself until ten years later, but when I did, I made sure to put children like me right in there, riding horses, wearing those amazing frocks, and mostly having adventures, just like everyone else.

Set My Senses Alight
Sue Lawson

When I was growing up, our family had "treasures" that were to be treated with reverence: the vase Dad gave Mum before they were married; my grandfather's massive carved wooden chair, not unlike a king's throne; a rare photo of my mum's father; Dad's stuffed pheasant. And books.

Not any particular book; all books.

Books were as much a part of our lives as food, water, and sunshine.

While I can remember lectures when playing, or later vacuuming, near Papa's chair and threats of death or worse if I strayed near that poor bird forever frozen midstep, I don't remember my parents ever spelling out that books had to be treated with respect. We four kids just knew they were treasures, filled with adventures, incredible worlds, new friends and old.

In the evening, while we watched television, Dad would read — book in his left hand, cigarette in his right.

Friday afternoons, Mum took us to the local library to borrow five books each. The memory of the weight of the library door, the smell of books, and the warmth of the sunshine streaming through the windows onto the children's book display are still vivid.

At home, we had a small room called "the Den," which at various times was a television room, a kids' playroom, and a bedroom.

When it was a TV room and playroom, I loved the Den. Not because of the closeted, safe feeling, the cool stonework surrounding the fireplace, or the front door that opened onto the rose- and camellia-filled garden.

I loved the Den because of the built-in, ceiling-to-floor bookshelves on either side of the fireplace.

From the mantelpiece down on the left-hand side were "our" books — picture books, novels, nursery rhymes, and poetry. There were books by Enid Blyton, A. A. Milne, May Gibbs, Dorothy Wall, Dr. Seuss, Lewis Carroll, Susan Coolidge, Bill Peet, Beatrix Potter, and many more.

The shelves above these held Mum and Dad's coffee-table books. A heavy tome filled with photos of JFK's life, Banjo Paterson's *Waltzing Matilda*, *Australia's Heritage*, and all manner of gardening books.

The right-hand side of the fireplace was overflowing with adult books: Flashman, Bond, shooting and cricket books, plus a few racy Harold Robbins and Jackie Collins books. Harold and Jackie were relegated to the very top shelf. (Accessible if you stood on the arm of the easy chair and held the mantelpiece for balance. Of course, I'm guessing that's the maneuver. I'd *never* do anything as evil as that.)

If ever I was stupid enough to use the word *bored* around Mum or Dad, I was directed to the Den to read.

If it was too wet to play in the garden or around the farm, I'd sit, back against the front door, and read.

If I needed to escape from whatever family or sibling trouble was brewing, I retreated to the Den to select a book.

I am who I am today because of those books, particularly.

Farewell to Shady Glade by Bill Peet introduced me to the importance of our environment. I returned to Milton Shulman's *Preep: The Little Pigeon of Trafalgar Square* again and again, even as a teenager, for the comfort it provided. Nancy Drew's adventures showed me that girls could be daring, clever, and still, well, girls. Dr. Seuss introduced me to the idea that words and nonsense were fun, except for *The Cat in the Hat.* That cat's antics stressed me out.

Leon Uris's *QB VII* and *Mila 18* taught me empathy and showed me the best and worst of humanity. However, deciding to read them in the lead-up to my Third Form (Year Nine) biology exam instead of actually studying wasn't my wisest choice.

My first love was a book character—Sodapop from *The Outsiders,* by S. E. Hinton. After I finished reading John Irving's *The World According to Garp,* I knew I wanted to, no, *needed* to write. I can remember when I finished the book, I dragged my portable Olivetti typewriter out from under the bed and bashed out a letter to Irving. I never did send it, but I do remember typing that his book, the characters, particularly Garp, and the way Irving used words had left me awed and reawakened my forgotten love of writing. Somewhere between graduating as a teacher and reading Garp, bands and music had absorbed me. Garp was a reminder of the power of story.

However, the book that not only inspired, terrified, and enthralled me but also changed me is the Australian young adult novel *Displaced Person* by Lee Harding.

I can't remember how I stumbled upon it in the school library. Perhaps the librarian, Mrs. Pelcan, directed me to it, or maybe I spied it when I was gossiping with friends between the fiction shelves. What I do know is that I've never forgotten how that book made me feel and how it has influenced how I write.

Displaced Person is about seventeen-year-old Graeme Drury, an ordinary kid doing ordinary things in Melbourne, and more specifically, St. Kilda.

Graeme is doing okay at school, has friends and a girlfriend, and is as happy as any teenager is at home.

However, Graeme starts to notice that his friends at school, people on the street, tram conductors, and McDonald's staff just don't see or hear him. Eventually, even his girlfriend and parents look straight through him. In no time Graeme's friends, girl-friend, and parents live their lives as though he never existed. Graeme also realizes that not only are people unable to see or hear him, but the world around him is fading to gray. He stumbles across the occasional object and a few people, and discovers that he, like them, is displaced.

I won't tell you any more or I'll ruin the story, and honestly, you need to read it.

It certainly wasn't the first book to move me; I mean, I fell in love reading *The Outsiders, Mila 18* showed me the astounding resilience of the human spirit, and *Lord of the Flies* taught me the importance of being true to your own principles even in the face of great danger.

But *Displaced Person* was something else again. This was a story about my world, and about me. It felt like it had been written for me. The places Graeme went, including the "displaced" houses, were familiar. I could picture the streets around St. Kilda and the houses with gum trees and rosebushes bowed under the weight of their blooms. I could smell the ocean and hear the seagulls as they squabbled on St. Kilda beach. The book set my senses alight.

Though I'd read dozens of Australian books before, *Displaced Person* was something else. Sure, when I read *Seven Little Australians*, I imagined the paddocks to be like our own, and every koala at Halls Gap made me think of Blinky Bill and mayhem — but while I was reading *Displaced Person*, the connection felt more "real."

For the first time, a book reached right into me and addressed my deepest fear — that I was insignificant, so ordinary that if I disappeared, no one would notice or miss me. It reflected my feeling that I was unable to impact, change or influence the world around me.

Displaced Person evoked an emotional response that I still feel when I think of the book. That is the power of a great story.

Perhaps my reaction to the book says more about the insecure, angst-ridden teenager I was, but even if that is the case, this book changed how I read and wrote.

Prior to reading *Displaced Person*, my own stories were superficial in the sense that I never crawled beneath my characters' skin.

After reading Lee Harding's book, throughout my twenties and between seeing bands at pubs — oh and teaching — I began experimenting, trying different points of view, structures, and styles. I began writing about difficult emotions — death, anxiety, depression, and belonging — from deep inside my characters. For a while I even tried writing poetry, but I quickly discovered that, while I love reading poetry, I truly suck at writing it.

Trust me, none of these stories and especially the poems were fantastic. In fact, I remember them as being pretty damn ordinary and filled with purple prose. But they were the beginnings of my writing journey, the spark that influenced how I write even now. Though at the time, I had no idea of the book's far-reaching effect; all I knew was I loved it.

It's only now, as an older and wiser writer, that I recognize and understand the profound effect *Displaced Person* has had upon my writing and the topics I tackle.

I don't write science fiction, but I do write realism and tackle meaty topics like depression, grief, and death in *You Don't Even Know*, the extensive impact of mental illness in *Pan's Whisper*, and racism and acceptance in *Freedom Ride*.

I can see now that my courage to tackle these issues, and to write in a familiar world about characters who are just like the students and people I met every day, started after I read *Displaced Person*.

Several years ago I managed to track down a copy and read it again. It didn't disappoint. It really is a wonderful book.

It's now on my bookshelf alongside *Preep*, *Farewell to Shady Glade*, *The World According to Garp*, *Hills End* (the bull in that story scared me stupid!), and *A Wrinkle in Time*, all books that had a profound effect upon me as a person and as a writer.

...mnrf...can't talk... gnrr...

Happy Endings
Brigid Lowry

I was a quiet, solemn child who lived with my three older sisters, my parents, and a bantam hen. My mother and father were bohemians, intellectuals, poor, charming, and interesting. They were also alcoholics. It was a messy, troubled childhood. Sometimes there were fabulous parties with dancing and laughter; sometimes there was shouting, violence, and neglect. We lived on the edges of happiness and craziness in the house at One Tree Hill, a place of polished floors, dusty corners, and secrets. Pink tea roses climbed in the windows; there was a grapefruit tree and a veggie garden, and for a too-brief while we looked after a spaniel with gentle floppy ears for an artist who'd gone to India. There were many books in our house: novels, communist magazines, poetry books, picture books, fairy tales, and photography books. I pored for hours over *The Family of*

Man, a collection of photographs from an exhibition by Edward Steichen at the Museum of Modern Art in New York. New York! Imagine! The photographs were of people of every age and nationality, doing all manner of things from being born to dying. I was beginning to learn that the world was much bigger than me, much stranger than my conventional school, and that it contained horizons far beyond my difficult family and my lonely bedroom.

My father was a printer who had a creative genius for typography and for being charming at the pub, but no talent for money. He would, for example, finish designing a wonderful poster for a symphony concert the day after the concert. My mother wrote poetry, drank too much sherry, and talked on the telephone late at night to someone who wasn't my father.

How I loved reading. Books were escape, solace, stimulation, a place of beauty and wonder. Books were important. They held the currency of ideas. Books were what you got for Christmas, if you were lucky. Books were carried home safely from my weekly expeditions to the Epsom Library, where you had to be Very Quiet. I withdrew as many books as I was allowed and devoured them, sprawled on my bed with my bantam at my feet for company. Books were to be respected. You had to look after books and not write on them or get them wet. They could be loaned but must always be given back. A book, I discovered, was also something you could write. I composed two poems, one about gypsies and one about autumn leaves, and my father printed a hundred copies, which I sold to unsuspecting relatives for two and sixpence each. I liked writing things down and carried a small hardback notebook with a dusty orange cover in which I wrote down quotes and things that interested me.

I enjoyed school. There were heaps of books at school. Books of maps, books of words, books of tidy letters. At school there was order, of a sort. Desks were in neat rows. Assembly came first; maths came after geography. After lunch, on sleepy afternoons, the teacher read us a chapter about Pegasus, the flying horse. I liked art, with its colors and paintbrushes, and I liked learning about foreign lands, but I liked English the best. English was easy; you got praise if you spelled *necessary* and *Mississippi* correctly. I liked dictation, where the teacher read something aloud and you had to write it down, and comprehension, in which you read something, then answered questions that proved you understood it.

In English, words were considered important. They reigned supreme. Both of these were good words: *reigned* and *supreme*. I collected words in my notebook. *Vanilla. Obfuscate. Jitterbug. Moonbeam.*

I would read anything, including books that were far beyond my reach, but I had favorite books which I read over and over again. One of them was *Bunchy* by Joyce Lankester Brisley, about a little girl living with her kindly grandmother, who cooked delicious treats. In each chapter Bunchy entered a different world where inanimate objects came to life: bread dough, scribbles, buttons, a snow dome, a decoupage screen, clothes pegs, magazine advertisements. They became elegant people to whom interesting things happened. I loved the imagination and creativity of this book, and the wonderful illustrations by the author. My own grandmothers were disappointing in comparison; one lived far away and the other was very sensible and stern. No magical characters came to life at my gran's house. Even though she was wealthy, she bought dry day-old cakes and required silence and obedience from her visiting grandchildren. Once I pinched a

185

sixpence from the neat pile in the kitchen, with which she bought the newspaper, and was forbidden to visit her for months. No doubt she loved her grandchildren, but it was a very restrained love.

Another favorite book was a New Zealand children's classic by Joyce West, called *Drovers Road*, set on a sheep station on the South Island. It featured Gay and Merry, who had spiffing times and rollicking good adventures on their delightful horses. My life was tricky, but between the pages of *Drovers Road*, I found safety and was soothed. In books, everything that went wrong got sorted out neatly. Loose ends were tidied; endings were happy. All was well, in books.

My most beloved book when I was eight was *The Good Master* by Kate Seredy. I liked it in the same way I liked anything from a foreign land: kimonos, Chinese woodcuts, sandalwood fans. *The Good Master* contained gypsies, snow, horses, spicy sausages, a fair, a kind uncle and aunt, a splendidly happy ending. I loved it because when I read it, I wasn't me anymore, a scared child in a house of disaster. I was Hungarian. I was Kate, riding her wild horse, playing with my new cousin, beloved of my aunt and uncle, in an exciting, exotic world.

Fifty years later, I'm asked to write about a book that meant something to me when I was young. *The Good Master*, I decide. It's not in the library, but it's still in print, so I order it online from America. With a click of my finger, the very reasonable sum of $11.95 disappears from my bank account, and a fortnight later my childhood book magically appears in my letter box. I leave it on the sofa for a day or two. I'm afraid to open it, in case it disappoints me. But once I dive in, it is pure pleasure. This is a paperback version, so it no longer has a dark-red leathery cover, but it still has the same gorgeous ink pictures by the author: Kate hiding in the rafters among the sausages, Kate and Jancsi riding their horses, skirts with eighteen petticoats, beautiful carved boxes made by a shepherd. Its themes are ecology, family, work, love, redemption. It praises living simply, and values education and love and goodness. It tastes of goulash and homemade spicy sausages. It tastes of happy.

When I was nine, my mother gave up on her marriage and shifted out on my father without telling him. We went to live in a vibrant inner-city suburb. My father, left alone in the big old house on the hill, gave up on everything, and a few weeks later, he took his own life. I grew older; I grew up; I tried every job I could think of: waitress, bookshop assistant, lab technician, primary-school teacher. I worked as a foster care worker; I lived in a Buddhist community; I got married and had a son. At thirty-five, after a challenging day as a relief teacher at a difficult school, I asked myself what I most loved doing. Writing was the answer, so I went back to university. I began by writing poetry and semi-autobiographical material, but I ended up writing *Guitar Highway Rose,* a book for teenagers that became a big success. I followed it with seven more titles for young adults, and my first book for adults is about to make its way into the world. In my books the world is a safe place. Stuff happens, but it's mainly good stuff. I try to accentuate the positive, the quirky, the kind. I write happy endings and leave others to write the dark, the heavy, and the disturbing. No surprises here.

I still love books. I give them as gifts for Christmas; I bring home as many as I can carry from the library. I'm looking forward to sharing books and stories, magic and adventures, ideas and creativity with my granddaughter. I'll introduce her to Eeyore and Piglet. I'll read her *Green Eggs and Ham* and *Where the Wild Things Are.* When she's older, I'll give her a copy of *The Good*

Master, written in 1935 but still as vibrant and relevant now as it was then. "I loved this when I was a kid," I'll say. I will give her books for Christmas, and I pray she won't be too busy on a screen to read them. I'll hug her like mad and cook her delicious things and let her make as much noise as she wants.

I'm growing my own wisdom.

You'll Go Blind: A Cautionary Tale About the Power of Reading
Julia Lawrinson

What I read as a child troubled me. Not everything, of course. There were uncomplicated experiences with Dr. Seuss, Little Golden Books, some version of Pooh Bear that barely resembled A. A. Milne's, and a book of poems I read until its cardboard cover shredded and the spine split.

But anything describing bodily ills preoccupied me.

My mother had a set of four medical encyclopedias, left over from two failed attempts at nursing. There were diagrams showing how to affix an arm sling, the features and effects of intestinal worms, and what a baby looks like in utero. There was a set of sketches featuring a hatted, long-coated man demonstrating what to do if caught in a nuclear explosion (dive into the gutter, put your hand behind your neck, don't look up), as well as pictures of how to best build and stock your bomb shelter. And, most affecting for me, there was a diagram of a young girl (me?) suffering the stages of polio, from sore throat and fever to stiff neck to hospitalization. Every time I got a sore throat (which was frequent: I grew up among smokers), I would anxiously assess my mother's eyes to see whether she, too, suspected I had the dread disease. If she thought my anxiety was odd, she never said anything. (If I'd had the courage to voice my fears, I'm sure she would have quickly informed me that I'd been immunized against polio at birth.)

Perhaps as a way to direct me away from gruesome medical specters, Mum gave me *Little House on the Prairie* when I was seven. The gift was inspired by the television series: before I got the books, I was already dressing like Laura, with long brown plaits, a long blue dress, and Wellington boots in lieu of lace-ups. Later, I tried to get Mum to knit me a pair of woolen stockings, but she said Perth was too hot. I also attempted to run down through the tricky, knotty weeds at the front of our house like it was a prairie. If my mother thought I was a bit odd, pretending to be a girl from the American Midwest in the 1870s, she never said anything.

The Little House books added a dimension to Laura's story that television could never hope to provide. I became obsessed with the details of their privations and setbacks, and I longed to suffer privations of my own. Perth and its suburban seventies tedium didn't seem adequate: I wanted Dad to hunt bears for our dinner and make our furniture out of saplings; I wanted Mum to invent new things to do with salted pork and cornmeal. I longed to have a bath a mere once a week. (I wouldn't have gone so far as to be deprived of ABBA, though; I was quite attached to that most modern contraption, the record player.)

I also loved the fact that naughtiness was not an invention of the twentieth-century real-life friends I was already fond of collecting and trying to emulate. Laura, the heroine of the Little House books, couldn't help the naughty things she thought and occasionally did, in spite of the strap that awaited her whenever she was caught. When she slapped her annoyingly perfect, blond, pretty sister, Mary, across the face after Mary taunted Laura about her brown hair, I wanted to applaud from across the century that divided us. When she led snooty Nellie Olsen into the creek until leeches attached themselves to Nellie's delicate town-girl legs, I admired the ingenuity of her revenge. And later, when an older Nellie made a move on Laura's soon-to-be fiancé while the three of them were on a horse-and-buggy ride, and Laura "accidentally" made the horses bolt so the fiancé could see Nellie's true colors, I was pleased that despite the strictness of her upbringing, Laura's spirit was not diminished.

But aside from the pleasure of reading about ancient girl combat, the Little House books fed my continuing obsession with illness and its life-altering effects.

One of the central events in the Little House series, the one that separates the books about Laura's childhood from those of her adolescence, concerns scarlet fever.

I remember reading and rereading the beginning of *By the Shores of Silver Lake*, the book that marks the beginning of Laura's maturity. The book began describing how Laura's mother and three sisters had been ill with scarlet fever. Pa and Laura were looking after everyone by themselves, and Pa was worried about how to pay the doctor's bill. But the most shocking thing to me was the dramatic but understated news that the disease had left Laura's older sister, Mary, blind.

I had been introduced to the idea of living with blindness by two other books that I'd got from the Scholastic Book Club: one about Helen Keller, which had the Braille alphabet on the back, and one about her teacher, Annie Sullivan. But having the previously insufferably good Mary become blind induced me to try to imagine in detail what it would be like. What would I do if one day such a calamity happened to me?

To this end, I spent entire days pretending to be blind.

If my mother thought there was something odd about me sitting at the kitchen table, eating my toast and Vegemite with my eyes scrunched up, she never said anything. She also refrained from commenting when we went to the supermarket, as I felt my way up the aisles with outstretched hands. I might have cheated by opening one eye from time to time to make sure I wasn't going to collide with the cornflakes display, and to check out the satisfyingly baffled expressions on the faces of other shoppers—but I wanted to be prepared. I wanted to understand.

I grew up, but I never grew out of obsessively identifying with the books that most spoke to me. I never discussed this phenomenon with anybody, any more than I disclosed my childhood penchant for pretending to be blind. It was only later that I realized that I was experiencing one of the gifts of reading: the ability to identify with people whose experiences were far removed from our own, to inhabit the skin of another for a short, imaginative while.

I might not grope my way around Coles or Woolworths these days, but I am still careful with what I read. Books still trouble me; they get under my skin; they make me feel as if I am inhabiting the worlds I'm reading about. Because of this, you won't find any books about serial killers on my shelf, or novels featuring anything medical. And if you want to know what I'm reading at the moment, look closely: I'm sure it's still written all over my face.

I'm learning how to
make my own books!

Ingenious Decisions
Sue McPherson

I'd love to say I've been reading since four and my love of words entered my bloodstream the day I picked up my first book . . . but I'd be lying. Apart from school readers in kindergarten and a few worn Little Golden Books, I battled through primary and secondary education unmoved by the written word. No excuses; it just wasn't part of who I was back then. Sport, farm life, friends, family, and music were by far more interesting than sitting with a book. It may not sound proper or sophisticated enough, but I reckon my introduction to books via great yarns, the visual arts, and music definitely shaped my journey as a reader/writer/storyteller.

So many things have influenced me as a reader and writer. To reduce my influences down to one book is impossible. That's why I've chosen four.

Jolliffe's Outback
Cartoons and Australiana
By Eric Jolliffe
Started reading at age thirteen

Yep, you read right. This is a cartoon book full of witty, most times mad, funny cartoons reflecting outback Australia. What a winner!

Like many cartoon books, *Jolliffe's Outback* magazine didn't have many words, which was fine by me. One or two sentences told the story—that's all that was needed. The image did the rest. Put the two together and you had a full story right there in one. Simple but very effective. The lad could draw, he knew the bush, and he knew the people and critters that lived among it. Eric Jolliffe was a grand storyteller.

Jolliffe's Outback magazines were laugh-out-loud funny, simple, and relatable. And we couldn't wait for a new one to hit the newsagents. My dad, Ernie, had a great love for and affinity with the bush. He worked in and around the smell of eucalyptus, snow gums, and rich mountain soil his whole life. Dad had a mad sense of humor and freaky sense of comic timing. Dad cracked us up; he'd sit in his chair at night and flip through the magazine, giggling and eventually laughing so much that you'd think he'd keel over dead with a heart attack.

Mum, Faye, the grown-up, was a lot more conservative. She was a great cook—still is—she would sew our uniforms, knit and crochet jumpers for harsh winter months. In between playing house, Mum would also trap and skin rabbits and sell them for meat and skins, milk the cow, and keep a beautiful garden. Mum didn't get Jolliffe like the rest of us. No matter how many times

Dad tried to share a hilarious cartoon moment, Mum wasn't interested. After telling Dad he was a silly old goat, she'd walk away. This in itself had us in stitches.

Even though Eric Jolliffe had his critics, his humor, love of the outback, and his observation of the people who lived within it enhanced my love of storytelling. Jolliffe taught me the importance of great images and crisp action while using the least amount of words possible, a structure also significant when writing for the screen.

If you ever come across a *Jolliffe's Outback* magazine, hold on to the bugger. Not only are they funny, entertaining, and educational; they're also collectible.

Adam's Empire
Novel
By Evan Green
Acquired age fifteen, first read age twenty-four

Adam's Empire is epic, a great Australian story. It has everything: humor, drama, romance, and it's all set in the Australian outback.

So this is what happened. When I was a teenager, Mum subscribed me to the Doubleday Book Club. I hated reading, so I found her eagerness a total waste of time and money. Obviously she saw something I didn't. Once a week our mail was collected from the post office in town. *Adam's Empire* was a big package, a huge hardcover book. Dad loved reading, so he was on it straightaway. After work he would plow through each page day after day until finally he finished. Dad was blown away by the story. But no matter how hard he pushed me to read *Adam's Empire*, there was no way I was going to read that monster of a book. I had better things to do.

Twelve or thirteen years later, I was a student teacher at uni. Now, this is where things changed. To pass, I had to read fiction and complete a journal on each book. I squirmed and complained and squirmed some more until finally I snapped out of it, listened to the lecturer, and played the game. After reading twenty or so young adult books, I was actually starting to enjoy myself. Each story transported me to a different world, a different family, another complication that needed attention. I was hooked. I remember looking across the room to my bookshelf. *Adam's Empire* stood boldly in front of me, daring me to pick it up. From the moment I started reading, Evan Green had me. And just like Dad years earlier, I read day and night until the book was finished.

It's a strong, relatable, and generous-with-detail type of story. To me, *Adam's Empire* does and has everything a good book should. Evan Green was another master storyteller, no doubt about it. He planted a seed so eager to grow, every spare dollar I had was spent on books. From then on I became a loyal member of the local library, consuming up to three books at the same time. From a nonreader to a book monster—who would have thought?

Believe it or not, I continue to read this book at least once a year.

The Book Thief
Novel
By Markus Zusak
Read after its release

Not only a great book but now a movie. What a legend, Markus Zusak.

As a reader, the story of *The Book Thief* was great, but as a *writer*, the story rocked my world. It just about sent my frizzy hair straight. It was the concept of Death speaking that totally blew me away. I know it has been done before, but this is the first time I had experienced it.

And I'll be truthful: while reading the first few pages . . . I had no idea what was going on, absolutely no idea. At the time I was busy with other projects and hadn't read any reviews. I had no idea Death was telling the story. Yep, I'm pretty embarrassed by this confession, but no worries — it all worked out; *The Book Thief* changed me.

I didn't study creative writing at uni, so I assumed that when writing you had to work within a set of boundaries. Having Death tell your story totally disintegrated that notion. What a revelation.

See, I don't like the idea of fitting inside a box. If I can change things up or out, I'm in my happy. Delivering a story that challenges and teases your own beliefs is very appealing. Thanks to Death and Markus's ingenious decisions as an author, I now have a healthier confidence in how I approach and tell a story. I'll seek out a story from all its angles, including the plot, characters, the environment, and the story's tone.

Ruby Moonlight
Verse novel
By Ali Cobby Eckermann
Read on its release, 2012, age forty-four

Ruby Moonlight is another great Australian story, about an Aboriginal woman living in the late nineteenth century.

So here it is: I didn't get poetry. Yeah, I know. Age forty-four, a published author, with no connection to poetry. Not a good look, eh? I understood the simple structure of rhyme, but other than that, I was totally lost. I had no idea what a narrative poem was. And to be honest, I would never have gone out of my way to find one. I figured I didn't have the poetry gene, full stop, end of story. Well, that was until I read *Ruby Moonlight*.

Talk about an onion; I peeled back so many skins after reading this gem that I knew I was changed as a storyteller. No more playing around the surface; I'm going to dive deeper, and this time I'll open my eyes. Ruby is very relatable; she's from the bush, she understands the bush, and she's Aboriginal. The writing is beautiful and intelligent. I love surprises; *Ruby Moonlight* offered many.

Now I can show you where the poetry section of our local library and bookshop is. I even have a poetry section in my own bookcase. And dare I say it? I even try to write my own poetry. Sweet Mary and Joseph, old girl here has finally found the light.

I don't know if it's timing, maturity, or both. Whatever the reason, I'm grateful poetry has entered my life. Connecting with poetry is another profound experience that has and will continue to shape my work as an author and screenwriter.

You know, I used to get embarrassed when asked about reading as a child, and then I thought, Well, you know what? I can't be the only one who didn't fall in love with books at an early age. Story is gold. Whether you read it, hear it as a yarn, in a song or melody, see it in a photo, canvas, in the sand, on a cave wall, in sculpture, or on the screen, it doesn't matter. Story is gold.

All four writers and their work have in some way made me a better storyteller. My introduction to books may have been delayed and unconventional, but it has worked for me. I look forward to hearing, reading, and watching your stories.

Knock yourselves out and get creative.

P.S. Just for the record, all of these books have dog-ears, small rips, and are stained with tea and coffee. Whatever their appearance, they are loved and treasured.

James Remembering
James Roy

When I was a young boy of around eleven or twelve, my family left Australia and went to live in Fiji. *Live in* Fiji. We weren't staying at some holiday resort with a kids' club and snorkeling, or even experiencing one of those trendy, eco-friendly village stays, but actually *living* there. Sounds great, doesn't it? And it was. Of course it was. That emotion you're feeling right now? Envy.

Here's the thing about Fiji. It's the kind of place where kids can play, and I mean *really* play. I don't think kids play the same way they used to, but we can talk about that another time. Right now, my point is that if a child of eleven or twelve wanted to do a lot of playing, Fiji would be just the kind of place to do it.

My father was a teacher at Fulton College, a missionary college where young people from all over the Pacific came to learn how to be teachers, ministers, or accountants. Fulton College was about fifty kilometers north of Suva and was surrounded by rolling hills, dairy farms, bamboo forests, bunya trees, thick jungle, rivers, creeks, and beaches. In other words, exactly the kind of adventuresome place where a kid can not just play, but *really* play. Serious, military-issue play.

But as anyone who knows anything about children in general—and about children's books in particular—can tell you, all the adventuresome places in the world are of very little use to someone unless there is another someone. Which is where Shannon enters the scene.

My cousin Shannon was—is—a couple of years younger than me, but as boys we really formed a connection. Lifelong, as it turned out. Part of this was around books, part of it was around play, but almost all of it was around the place where books and play met. We lived in the shaded part of a vast books/play Venn diagram. We would read adventure books like, say, *The Adventures of Tom Sawyer,* or *The Adventures of Huckleberry Finn,* or *Swallows and Amazons,* and then, with those books forming a kind of script to our play, we would *become* Tom and Huck, or the crew of *Swallow.* Or if not those exact kids, then characters very much like them.

Shannon owned a very impressive library of children's books. Mine was slightly less impressive. At least it was until the day my father came home from the post office with a big box from his university back in Australia. He was studying for his master of education degree and was about to begin a children's literature unit.

I helped him open the box, and as shafts of golden light burst forth (this is how I remember it), I saw that contained within was a rather impressive and totally instant library of children's books. For me. And for Shannon, too, of course, but mostly for me.

Okay, so they weren't technically *mine*, but that didn't prevent me from taking the entire contents of that box to my room, clearing a shelf of my bookcase, and lining them up, ready to tackle one at a time.

Several of the books in that box would end up as lifelong favorites. *The Nargun and the Stars* by Patricia Wrightson; *Midnite* by Randolph Stow; *A Wrinkle in Time* by Madeleine L'Engle; *Cue for Treason* by Geoffrey Trease; *Smith* by Leon Garfield. (*The Lion, the Witch and the Wardrobe* was in there, too, but since Shannon already owned the full set of Narnia books, that one was old news.) *The Mouse and His Child* by Russell Hoban was another definite highlight, and now slots in at number two on my personal hit parade of books.

I remember putting one particular book aside simply because it looked . . . well, kind of boring, to be honest. The image on the front was a washed-out watercolor of a scrawny kid being jostled along by a bunch of sandy-headed boys. It was written by Ivan Southall, and the only book of his I'd previously read had left me underwhelmed. Even the title of this one seemed to be struggling for something interesting to say.

Josh.

Not *Josh Gets Jostled* or *Josh Has a Crappy Day* or even *Josh Goes to Stay with His Weird Aunt Clara and Has a Ghastly Time of It.* Just plain *Josh.*

That book lay to one side for some time, while I charged like a kid possessed through everything else on that shelf. So many great books! A few duds as well, but mostly good. Lots of good books, and the boring, watercolor excuse for a kids' book that I couldn't bring myself to read.

But eventually—mostly because it was made of words, I guess—I picked up *Josh,* opened it, and began to read.

If you don't mind, I'm now going to give you a bit of background to the book. I'll try not to include any spoilers, but if I do see one coming I'll be sure to let you know well in advance.

Josh Plowman is a city boy, born and bred. He's part of an enormous network of cousins, most of whom have told him that if you want to be considered a proper Plowman, you have to go and stay with Aunt Clara in Ryan Creek. Why? Because that's what Plowman kids do. Ryan Creek was basically *started* by Great-grandfather Plowman. He built the famous old timber bridge — everyone knows that. If you're a Plowman, then you're Ryan Creek royalty.

Josh doesn't want to be royalty, especially not in a one-horse town like Ryan Creek. It's not his style. He just likes reading books and writing poetry. He knows nothing of life in the country, and doesn't really care to learn. But he senses down deep that he *has to do it.* After all, he can't call himself a proper Plowman until he has! He can't fit into his own family unless he has gritted his teeth and faced up to his scary old meddling aunt, and to the big, nasty, bullying country boys who want to kill him with a cricket ball. Or by drowning him under the old bridge that Great-grandfather Plowman built.

(Sorry, that was a bit of a spoiler. Just so you know, he doesn't die. But it does get pretty hairy for a while there.)

Now, having considered Josh Plowman, it's time to consider me, just for a moment. Not 2016 me, but 1981 me. The timid young missionary kid living in a place he doesn't really know, a place where he doesn't entirely fit in. A place that oftentimes causes him to wish he could just go home.

Everyone knows that often the best books are the ones that speak to us, the ones that we truly relate to. The ones that make us go, "I know that feeling." Usually they're the books that also make us feel okay about our own experiences. When we see a character who is scared, or alone, or stupidly in love, or being unreasonably jealous, it makes us feel just that little bit better about the times *we've* felt that way. That's kind of the point, I think, especially in books for young people.

For me, *Josh* was that book. It wasn't the only book that did that for me, but it was the one that spoke to me the most clearly.

Ivan Southall had one more surprise in store for me, a surprise that contributed to my desire to be a writer. I could name several other books which more directly stoked that fire, but *Josh's* role was still important, especially in influencing the *kind* of writer I would become. This was thanks to a number of sentences in general, but to one sentence in particular. What we will call *The Sentence*.

First, the many sentences. I have this sneaking suspicion that *Josh* might have been the first Australian verse novel for young readers. Long before Steven Herrick, Catherine Bateson, and others were using free narrative verse to tell longer stories, Ivan Southall had already done it. Not that the text of this book *looks* very much like verse. But many of the same devices are there: internal narrative; stream of consciousness; short, highly distilled phrases that pack a serious wallop.

Which *almost* brings me to The Sentence, and I promise to get to it very soon.

When I was in primary school, English was taught a little differently. We had the spelling and the comprehension and the "composition" (just a fancy word for what we now call "creative writing" or "narrative writing"), but we also learned grammar. Proper "name the subject, predicate, and conjunction in this sentence" grammar. Underline the participial phrase. Put a circle around the locational preposition. Then we were tested on it. I know, right?

These days the word processor on your computer will tell you when a sentence isn't right. In most cases it does this with a green squiggly line and some comment, such as *Sentence fragment—consider revising.* Back then, in the seventies and eighties, you just had to *know* that stuff.

I found those rigid rules kind of annoying. I understood that there was a need for grammatical guidelines, mostly to stop society from drifting back to communicating with grunts and confused looks. But at the same time I was starting to stretch my wings as a creative writer, without being quite sure how bendy those rules were, or could be.

So imagine my surprise—and elation—when I read this paragraph, right near the end of chapter 35, closely followed by The Sentence.

Josh trying to find a bottom to stand on, nothing to hang on to, nothing to put his feet on, nothing but water and darkness and no breath to breathe with.
Josh drowning.

Two words. *Josh drowning.* No green squiggly line, just one perfect "incomplete" sentence. Matter-of-fact. No embellishment. Direct. Terrifying.

Yes, I clearly remember reading The Sentence and thinking, Aha! I knew it! Rules can be bent, even snapped in half! Oh, happy day! I just *knew* we were overcomplicating this stuff!

So, now I'm a writer. I hope that one day I'll be good enough to win the most prestigious children's literature prize in the world—the Carnegie Medal. It's only been done once before by an Australian writer—by Ivan Southall, for *Josh*.

But that's not why I love this book. The fact that *Josh* won the Carnegie is not why I value it so highly. After all, most young readers couldn't care less about things like book prizes. They just want a good story. Don't they?

They want a story that they can relate to.

They want a story that makes them feel something they recognize, something that makes them feel better about being who they are, about being the way they are, and, sometimes, about *where* they are.

For me, *Josh* was that book.

Seeing Red
Jaclyn Moriarty

When I was six years old, a girl named Angela called out to the school playground: "If you think you've been invited to my birthday party, come and stand here!"

Everyone ran and lined up in front of her. Angela's family lived in a flat above the local newsagency, so she was the most popular girl in the class. To be invited to her party—to actually see the home above the newsagency, at the same time as eating fairy bread—well, the idea took your breath away. Nobody in that line was breathing.

Angela was holding a stack of white envelopes. As each person reached the front, she checked the stack and either handed over an envelope or shook her head. Some kids were already weeping. Some had been given envelopes and were celebrating noisily, which seemed insensitive to me. I got to the front of the line.

Angela flipped through the pile. She hesitated. She went through again. *She gave me an envelope.*

I stepped away, light-headed. There was the weight of the envelope in my hand, the brightness of that white. *Jacky,* it said, which was not how I spell my name. I had a moment of uneasiness about that but let it go. People never spell my name right. I was used to it. I had an invitation. I began to tear it open.

Then I sensed a kerfuffle in the line. It was breaking up. Angela had moved away, and people were crowding her, "Wait! You haven't finished giving them out!" but she was pushing through. She was heading for me. She was reaching over. She was pulling the envelope out of my hand.

"This is for Jacky *B*!" she said. "Not you! Sorry!"

I stared at my empty hands. The sound of Jacky B whooping reached me through a haze.

Also when I was six years old, I liked to pretend I was a circus performer. I walked along the school benches, balancing. These were made of evenly spaced wooden slats. Usually, I slipped and fell through a gap between slats. My leg would get caught. I'd be trapped there for whole lunchtimes. Eventually, Sister Rosalia, the teacher, would come and rescue me by rubbing my leg with warm soapy water. A day or so later, I'd decide to try again.

A girl in my class, Christine W, took an interest in me. She was exactly twice my height. Or anyway, I came up to her shoulder. She liked to squeeze the back of my neck, or slap my arm, or twist my wrist. It all seemed to delight her.

That was the year my mother gave me a pear for little lunch every day. The juice would dribble down my sleeves. I'd get pear juice everywhere. It really depressed me. One day, there was a butterfly cupcake in my bag instead of the pear. I walked toward the playground, holding it before me, admiring the swoop of those cake-wings, the rich red of the jam, astonished.

There was a rush of soft darkness and my butterfly cupcake was gone.

Sammy, the class dog, had eaten it right out of my hand.

"Well, what did you think would happen, holding a cupcake in front of a dog like that?" cried Sister Rosalia.

Our school library was a small dark room. There was a wall of books and a table. One day, I pulled out a book called *The Magic Finger* by Roald Dahl.

I sat at the table to read it.

It's the story of a girl who has a secret. Whenever she feels angry, her finger starts to tingle. A flash of light jumps out of her and lands on the person who made her angry, and things begin to happen....

When the family next door goes out hunting, ignoring the girl's pleas to stop, her Magic Finger tingles—and turns them into a family of ducks.

I loved the book. It was funny and took unexpected turns.

But the thing that made the world close to a point for me, while I was reading it, was this: the girl kept saying, "I saw red."

I had never heard the expression before. I figured out, from the context, that it had something to do with anger, but it seemed to me that it also meant more than that. It was such a strange, puzzling, evocative phrase, so empty and yet so full at the same time.

The year that I was six, I had a terrible secret.

When Angela swiped the invitation from my hand, when I was trapped in the school bench, when Christine slapped me, when the dog ate my butterfly cake—I felt rage.

My rage was very specific: I wanted to become a giant and use my giant foot to smash things.

But I was a good girl. A very, very good girl. My goodness took the form of being quiet. When I wasn't stuck in a bench, Sister Rosalia loved me! Because I was so nice and quiet! She was always giving me holy cards for sitting quietly with my arms folded. I was so quiet, I got left behind in classrooms. I was so quiet, people thought I was just moving my lips when I spoke.

A teacher asked me a question in the playground once. When I answered, she leaned in close. "You're a little mouse," she said. "Listen to you. Little mouse."

I stared at her. I imagined how she would look flat as a pancake underneath my giant boot.

I told nobody about my fury. It scared me. It seemed important to keep it secret.

But when I read *The Magic Finger*, there it was. Here was a girl, around my own age, feeling immense, powerless rage. And the enormity of her anger was captured in a single, curious handful of words: I saw red.

I borrowed *The Magic Finger* from the library every single week for the rest of the year.

Yesterday, I googled the phrase "seeing red." The first few results said it was to do with waving red flags at bulls (although bulls are actually agitated by the movement of the flag, not its color, since they can't see red). Other sites speculated that the phrase refers to the bloodshot eyes, or even the "red aura," of angry people.

Then I found a site that asked whether people might *literally* see red. I scrolled down, through comment after comment from people who said that they do. These people described feeling infuriated — a boy had been attacked by strangers; a woman had discovered that her dead son's possessions had been stolen — and then finding, briefly, that their entire world had turned red. As if they were seeing through cellophane or amber, they said, or from inside a red haze. Many also described a rushing sound in their ears, shaking hands, a sense of dissociation—and then a kind of extraordinary, superhuman strength. Some blacked out after seeing red and woke to find people staring at them in amazement, because they'd just floored three huge men, or destroyed a car. Many said that, while the world was tinted with red, they'd never felt so strong: that time slowed down, they were invincible. And then, they said, the anger fell away, and they were left exhausted, themselves again.

I reread *The Magic Finger* today. For a story about rage, it's surprisingly gentle. It's mainly about the family next door spending the night as ducks. They fly, build a nest, get hungry, and look for food. (The kids are horrified at the idea of eating worms. Their mother offers to mince the worms up into "worm burgers" or "slug burgers." They decide to eat apples instead.) It rains in the night and the family is cold, wet, and miserable; the next day they find themselves the targets of hunters.

It's not a story of revenge or punishment. It's not violent or vindictive. It's just a family of hunters finding out exactly how it is to be a duck: to live like ducks, and to be shot at.

In the end they turn back into people. They vow never to hunt again. They smash their guns to pieces, they scatter barley for ducks, and they change their name from the Greggs to the Eggs, in honor of all birds.

The girl is relieved that the family is okay: she never knows what her Magic Finger will do when she is angry and, as mad as she was about their hunting, she didn't want them to get hurt. But this time, what her magic has done is to change her neighbors by helping them see the truth.

The Magic Finger snared me by knowing my secret about

anger and by capturing the secret in a single mysterious phrase. But maybe it kept me mesmerized so long because it turned the secret into something good. The girl in the book did not lose control and disappear into a rampage. Instead she discovered a power in herself, to change things by making people see.

Years after I had read *The Magic Finger*, I was doing an honors degree in English literature. I couldn't decide whether to do my thesis on Virginia Woolf or F. Scott Fitzgerald. I woke in the night and decided that it should be on Roald Dahl. My thesis supervisor thought I'd lost my mind. "I'll do a post-structural analysis of *Charlie and the Chocolate Factory*!" I told him. "I'll write about Dahl from the perspective of Foucault!"

Neither of us knew what I was talking about.

"This is a mistake," he said, but he suggested I write the first chapter of a Roald Dahl thesis and see how it went.

A few weeks later, I went to see him in his office. He was holding the first chapter.

He looked at me curiously. "You seem so nervous and uncertain in person," he said, "but this writing's like a force of nature. You've persuaded me. Keep going."

The point is this: you can be angry or unhappy, lonely or shy, but it's always better to make your voice heard, so that people see your truth, than to turn into a giant and crush them.

(I never went to Angela's birthday party, but she and I ended up friends. So I got to see the flat above the newsagency after all. Every time I visited, her dad used to give us free lollies from behind the counter. That was better than a party.)

Nobody can tell me what to think.

thankyou!

About the Authors

RANDA ABDEL-FATTAH is an award-winning author of young adult books and a human-rights and antiracism advocate. She is a regular guest at schools and international writers' festivals. Randa worked as a litigation lawyer for almost ten years but is now undertaking a PhD exploring everyday multiculturalism and Islamophobia. She lives in Sydney, Australia, with her husband and their three children.

BERNARD BECKETT lives in Porirua, New Zealand. He is a high-school drama teacher and the father of three young boys. He has written a number of novels and plays. His most recent novel, *Lullaby,* was published in 2015.

CATHY CASSIDY is the author of the Chocolate Box Girls series and many other books. She has worked as a teen-mag journalist, illustrator, agony aunt, and art teacher but now writes full-time. She lives with her husband, kids, and a houseful of unruly rescue animals in England.

FELICITY CASTAGNA's latest book, *The Incredible Here and Now*, received the Australian Prime Minister's Literary Award for Young Adult Fiction in 2014. Her work has been widely published in Australian literary magazines and newspapers and produced for radio. She teaches writing at arts centers, schools, and universities. She recently completed a PhD with the Writing and Society Research Centre at the University of Western Sydney.

QUEENIE CHAN was born in 1980 in Hong Kong and migrated to Australia when she was six years old. In 2004, she began drawing a three-volume mystery-horror series called the Dreaming for LA-based manga publisher Tokyopop. She has since collaborated on several graphic novels with author Dean Koontz for his Odd Thomas series and with Kylie Chan for her *White Tiger* fantasy series. She is currently working on book three of *Fabled Kingdom*, a fairy tale–inspired fantasy story. Apart from her professional work, she also draws a number of short stories on her personal website.

KATE CONSTABLE is a Melbourne writer who grew up in Papua New Guinea. She has written ten novels for children and young adults, including the award-winning *Crow Country*, the Chanters of Tremaris series, *Cicada Summer*, and *New Guinea Moon*. She still loves stories about time.

RACHAEL CRAW began her working life as an English teacher after completing a degree in classical studies and drama at the University of Canterbury, in new Zealand. She dabbled in acting, directing, and writing for amateur theater productions and small independent film ventures. Her passion for dialogue and characterization finally led to long-form writing with the Spark series. Rachael's enthusiasm for classical heroes, teen angst, and popular culture informs much of her creative process. She enjoys small-town life at the top of the South Island of New Zealand, where she lives with her husband and three daughters.

ALISON CROGGON is an award-winning poet whose work has been published extensively in anthologies and magazines internationally. So far she has written seven internationally released YA fantasies: the five-part series the Books of Pellinor, *Black Spring* (short-listed for the New South Wales Premier's Literary Award), and *The River and the Book*. She has written widely for theater, and her plays and opera libretti have been produced all around Australia. Alison is also an editor and critic. She lives in Melbourne, Australia, with her husband, Daniel Keene, a playwright.

CATH CROWLEY is an award-winning young adult author published in Australia and internationally. Her books include the Gracie Faltrain trilogy, *Chasing Charlie Duskin, Graffiti Moon,* and *Words in Deep Blue.* Cath writes and teaches in Melbourne, Australia.

TED DAWE has written four novels: *Thunder Road* (2003), *K. Road* (2005), *And Did Those Feet . . .* (2006), and *Into the River* (2012). He has also written a collection of short stories, *Captain Sailor Bird and Other Stories* (2007). He has received a number of awards, including the *New Zealand Post* Young Adult Book Award (twice), the *New Zealand Post* Best First Book, and the *New Zealand Post* Margaret Mahy Award for Book of the Year

(2013). In 2014 he was named an Honorary Literary Fellow by the New Zealand Society of Authors. He lives in Auckland, New Zealand, with his wife and son.

URSULA DUBOSARSKY wanted to be a writer from the age of six, and is now the author of more than forty books for children and young adults, which have won several national prizes, including the New South Wales, Victorian, South Australian, and Queensland Premiers' Literary Awards. She lives in Sydney, Australia, with her family.

SIMON FRENCH grew up in Sydney, Australia, and had his first children's novel published while he was still in high school. He has written novels and picture books, published in Australia and overseas. His work is praised by critics and has won several awards, including the 1987 Children's Book Council of Australia (CBCA) Book of the Year Award for *All We Know. Change the Locks* was a CBCA Honour Book in 1992. His novel *Where in the World* won the 2003 New South Wales Premier's Literary Award for Children's Literature and was short-listed for the 2003 CBCA Book of the Year for Younger Readers, long-listed for the 2003 *Guardian* Children's Fiction Prize, and nominated to the International Board on Books for Young People Honour List in 2004. *Other Brother* is his most recent novel for children. Simon is a primary-school teacher in the Hawkesbury region of New South Wales, Australia.

MANDY HAGER is a multi-award-winning New Zealand author for young adults. Her most recent book, *Singing Home the Whale,* won the 2015 *New Zealand Post* Young Adult Book Award and Margaret Mahy Award for Book of the Year, and was named to the 2016 International Board on Books for Young People Honour List. When she is not working on her own projects, she teaches novel writing and has just become a doting granny.

SIMMONE HOWELL spent her teen years writing love odes to eighties pop stars and English essays for her friends. She is the author of novels *Notes from the Teenage Underground, Everything Beautiful,* and *Girl Defective. Notes from the Teenage Underground* was awarded the 2007 Victorian Premier's Prize for YA fiction and the inaugural Inky Teenage Choice Award. *Everything Beautiful* was a finalist in the Melbourne Prize for Best Writing. *Girl Defective* was short-listed for the 2014 Prime Minister's Literary Award. Simmone lives in Melbourne, Australia, where she writes, drinks coffee, and dreams of faraway places.

CATHERINE JOHNSON is a born-and-bred Londoner who now lives on the South Coast of England and looks at the sea a lot. She studied film at Saint Martin's School of Art, in London. Her last novel, *The Curious Tale of the Lady Caraboo* has been nominated for the Carnegie Medal. She also writes for radio, film, and TV.

WILL KOSTAKIS writes for young adults and younger readers. His *The First Third* was short-listed for the Children's Book Council of Australia Book of the Year Award and won the Inside a Dog Gold Inky. His latest release is *The Sidekicks.* He still hasn't finished *Hatchet.*

AMBELIN KWAYMULLINA is an Aboriginal author, illustrator, and law academic who comes from the Palyku people of the Pilbara region of Western Australia. She is the author-illustrator of a number of award-winning picture books as well as the author of The Tribe books, a dystopian series for young adults.

BENJAMIN LAW is a Sydney-based journalist, columnist, and screenwriter, and has completed a PhD in television writing and cultural studies. He is the author of *The Family Law* (2010) and *Gaysia: Adventures in the Queer East* (2012), and co-wrote *Shit Asian Mothers Say* (2014) with his sister Michelle and illustrator Oslo Davis. Both his books have been nominated for Australian Book Industry Awards, and *The Family Law* has been adapted into a major TV series in Australia. Benjamin has also written for more than fifty publications, businesses, and agencies in Australia and worldwide.

JULIA LAWRINSON grew up in the outer suburbs of Perth, Australia, and spent her childhood rereading the limited number of books in her house, including Reader's Digest condensed novels, medical encyclopedias, and *Little House on the Prairie*. These days she writes novels for children and young adults, and revisits the Little House books from time to time, just to make sure they're still as good as they were.

SUE LAWSON's love for books and stories began when she was a child in country Victoria, Australia. On her family farm, she spent her time reading, writing, listening to her father's and grandfather's stories, and avoiding working with the cattle. Her young adult novels include *Pan's Whisper* and *You Don't Even Know*. Sue's latest book is *Freedom Ride*. (It's ironic that she only discovered after leaving the town where she'd lived for fourteen years that Lee Harding had been born there.)

BRIGID LOWRY is the award-winning author of eight young adult titles, including *Guitar Highway Rose* and *Juicy Writing: Inspiration and Techniques for Young Writers*. Brigid also writes poetry, essays, and performance pieces, and has an MA in creative writing. She believes in nectarines, colored pencils, and thrift shops, and in encouraging others to live with authenticity and joy. Her first adult book is *Still Life with Teapot: On Zen, Writing and Creativity*.

EMILY MAGUIRE is the author of five novels and two non-fiction books, and a teacher and mentor to emerging writers. She has twice been named as a *Sydney Morning Herald* Young Novelist of the Year. Her latest book is the novel *An Isolated Incident*.

CATHERINE MAYO has always been a compulsive reader and dreamer. She studied violin, history, philosophy, and geology before becoming a musician, violin maker, and restorer. Thirteen years ago she started writing and has won several prizes in short-story competitions. She is the author of the young adult novel *Murder at Mykenai* and its sequel, *The Bow*.

SUE McPHERSON grew up with her adoptive family on a property near Batlow, in southern New South Wales, Australia. Her first book, *Grace Beside Me*, was published in 2012. From her home in Eumundi, in Queensland, Australia, Sue continues to create and write stories either for publication or screen.

JACLYN MORIARTY is the author of several novels for young adults (and one for adults), including the internationally best-selling *Feeling Sorry for Celia* and *Finding Cassie Crazy*, and, most recently, the Colors of Madeleine trilogy. Her books have won several prizes, including the New South Wales Premier's Literary Award, the Queensland Literary Award, and the Aurealis Award for Best Young Adult Fantasy. A former media lawyer, Jaclyn grew up in Sydney, Australia, lived in the United States, the United Kingdom, and Canada, and now lives in Sydney again.

From the early 2000s till his death, in 2015, MAL PEET quietly gathered literary awards in the U.K., the United States, and Europe. Although he is best known as a writer of fiction for young adults, his books have a wide and growing adult readership. He was born in Norfolk, England, in 1947.

JUDITH RIDGE learned to read before she started school and hasn't stopped since. In between books, she has worked as a teacher, editor, critic, and writer, and on a range of projects and festivals designed to encourage young people to be readers and writers. She is internationally known for her expertise in children's and young adult literature and has spoken at conferences and festivals all around the world. Judith is currently writing her PhD on Australian children's and young adult fantasy fiction. She lives in a dusty old house in South Windsor, New South Wales, Australia, with two batty cats, and too many books.

JAMES ROY has written more than thirty books for children and young adults, some of which have medal stickers on the front covers. He visits more than fifty schools locally and abroad each year, and lives in the beautiful Blue Mountains near Sydney,

Australia, where he enjoys coaxing vaguely musical sounds out of a variety of instruments.

SHAUN TAN is an artist, a writer, and a filmmaker based in Melbourne, Australia. His illustrated books for both adults and children include *The Rabbits, The Red Tree, Rules of Summer, Tales from Outer Suburbia*, and the acclaimed wordless novel *The Arrival*. In 2011 he received the Astrid Lindgren Memorial Award and an Academy Award for his short animated film *The Lost Thing*.

DR. JARED THOMAS is a Nukunu person of Australia's Southern Flinders Ranges. Jared's play *Flash Red Ford* toured Uganda and Kenya in 1999, and his play *Love, Land and Money* was featured during the 2002 Adelaide Fringe Festival. Jared's young adult novel *Sweet Guy* was short-listed for the South Australian and Victorian Premiers' Literary Awards, and his children's novel *Dallas Davis, the Scientist and the City Kids* is part of the Oxford University Press Yarning Strong series. His latest novel, *Calypso Summer*, won the 2013 State Library of Queensland black&write! Indigenous Writing Fellowship, was short-listed in the 2014 Victorian Premier's Literary Award for Indigenous Writing, and joined the 2015 International Youth Library White Ravens List, a list of books that deserve worldwide attention because of their universal themes and exceptional artistic and literary style and design. His professional career has included roles such as manager of Aboriginal and Torres Strait Islander arts for Arts South Australia and lecturer at the University of South Australia.

FIONA WOOD is the author of *Six Impossible Things, Wildlife*, and *Cloudwish*. *Six Impossible Things* was short-listed for the

Children's Book Council of Australia (CBCA) Book of the Year, Older Readers, in 2011. *Wildlife* won the CBCA Award in 2014 and was short-listed for a number of other awards. *Cloudwish* won the 2016 Australian Indie Book Award for YA fiction and was long-listed for the 2016 Gold Inky Award. Her books are published internationally. Before writing YA fiction, Fiona wrote television scripts. She lives in Melbourne, Australia, with her family.

MARKUS ZUSAK is the author of five novels: *The Underdog, Fighting Ruben Wolfe, Getting the Girl, I Am the Messenger,* and *The Book Thief.*

About the Indigenous Literacy Foundation

The Indigenous Literacy Foundation (ILF) was founded by Suzy Wilson and set up by members of the Australian Book Industry in 2005 with the core aim of drawing upon the skills and expertise of the Australian book industry to address literacy levels in remote Indigenous communities.

The ILF aims to raise literacy levels and improve the lives and opportunities of Indigenous children living in remote and isolated regions. This is done through the delivery of books and literacy resources, publishing, and an early literacy program called Book Buzz. In addition, the Foundation advocates to raise community awareness of Indigenous literacy issues.

The Foundation is a not-for-profit charity, without any government or major corporate funding. It works with the support of the Australian Publishers Association, the Australian Booksellers Association, and the Australian Society of Authors, along with a team of ambassadors, volunteers, and four full-time staff.

The Foundation's major fund-raising campaign, the Great Book Swap, is held on Indigenous Literacy Day, the first Wednesday in September each year.

Books Mentioned
in the Collection

Writers Mentioned in the Collection

Joan Aiken

Catherine Bateson

The Brothers Grimm

Judy Blume

Lewis Carroll

Paul Celan

Aidan Chambers

Susan Coolidge

Jackie Collins

Caroline B. Cooney

Fyodor Dostoyevsky

Michel Foucault

Kenneth Grahame

Alan Garner

May Gibbs

Steven Herrick

Robin Klein

E. L. Konigsburg

Edward Lear

C. S. Lewis

Jan Mark

A. A. Milne

E. Nesbit

Charles Perrault

Christopher Pike

Beatrix Potter

Harold Robbins

Siegfried Sassoon

William Shakespeare

R. L. Stine

Dylan Thomas

Dorothy Wall

Jacqueline Wilson

William Wordsworth

Benjamin Zephaniah

Acknowledgments

T hank you to Sarah Foster and Nicola Robinson for getting things started, and to Mary Verney and the rest of the amazing team at Walker Books Australia for bringing it all together so beautifully. I am so very grateful to the contributors for sharing these delicious slices of their reading lives, and for their generosity in donating their author royalties to the Indigenous Literacy Foundation. Special thanks to Angelo Loukakis and Pamela Freeman for their personal and professional advice and support.

Copyright Acknowledgments